weird but true! 2024

Published by Collins
An imprint of HarperCollins Publishers
Westerhill Road
Bishopbriggs
Glasgow G64 2QT
www.harpercollins.co.uk

HarperCollins Publishers
Macken House, 39/40 Mayor Street Upper, Dublin 1, D01 C9W8, Ireland

In association with National Geographic Partners, LLC

NATIONAL GEOGRAPHIC and the Yellow Border Design are trademarks of
the National Geographic Society and used under license.

National Geographic Kids Weird But True & Design are trademarks of
National Geographic Society and used under license.

First published 2023

ISBN 978-0-00-861920-6

10 9 8 7 6 5 4 3 2 1

A catalogue record for this book is available from the British Library

Printed in UAE.

If you would like to comment on any aspect of this book, please contact
us at the above address or online.
natgeokidsbooks.co.uk
collins.reference@harpercollins.co.uk

Paper from responsible sources.

wild & wacky

facts & photos!

Contents

Amazing Earth

The **ARCHES OF ÉTRETAT,** in France, are so famous that they've been **PAINTED** by artists including **MONET** and have featured in **FILMS** and **BOOKS!**

Travel over to page 14 to see more effects of erosion.

Crossing the
CONTINENTS

ALL EARTH ▶

Once upon a time, all the land on Earth was joined together in a supercontinent called Pangaea. It began to split apart about 200 million years ago, during the age of the dinosaurs.

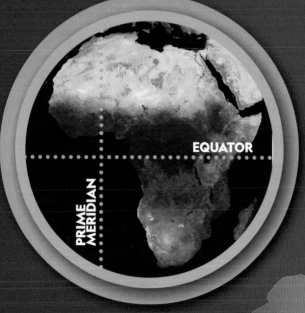

EQUATOR

PRIME MERIDIAN

◀ QUARTERS OF A CONTINENT

Africa is the only continent to cover all four hemispheres – northern, southern, eastern and western. The Equator splits Africa between north and south. Another invisible line known as the prime meridian divides east and west.

◀ GIANT JIGSAW

The shape of the continents still shows how they once fit together like a huge jigsaw puzzle. For example, the ins and outs of the east coast of South America would fit pretty neatly with the outs and ins of the west coast of Africa if you pushed them together!

THE LOST CONTINENT

Lying mostly underwater in the South Pacific Ocean is a huge area of continental crust called Zealandia. At over half the size of Australia, some scientists think that it should officially be the eighth continent.

▼

▲ A DIVIDED CITY

In Istanbul, Turkey, you can go shopping on two continents in a matter of minutes! A road bridge spans the Bosphorus Strait that separates the Asian and European sides of the city.

SMALLEST OR ▶ BIGGEST ?

An island is defined as a piece of land that's completely surrounded by water, but is smaller than a continent. Australia would be the largest island in the world – if it wasn't already the smallest continent.

The continents move at a speed of about 1.5 cm a year – that's about as fast as your toenails grow!

The middle of NOWHERE

In the **PACIFIC OCEAN**, far away from anywhere, is a place that **SCIENTISTS** call the **'OCEANIC POLE OF INACCESSIBILITY'**. It's better known as **POINT NEMO** – a word that means **'NO ONE'** in Latin, which gives you a clue to its **CLAIM TO FAME**.

Did you KNOW?

Point Nemo is named after Captain Nemo from the book *20,000 Leagues Under the Sea*, by Jules Verne.

Totally WEIRD!

In 1997, a really loud noise was recorded in this remote region of the Pacific. This mysterious sound was nicknamed the 'Bloop', and for years scientists wondered what it could be. Eventually, they realised it was the sound of icebergs cracking!

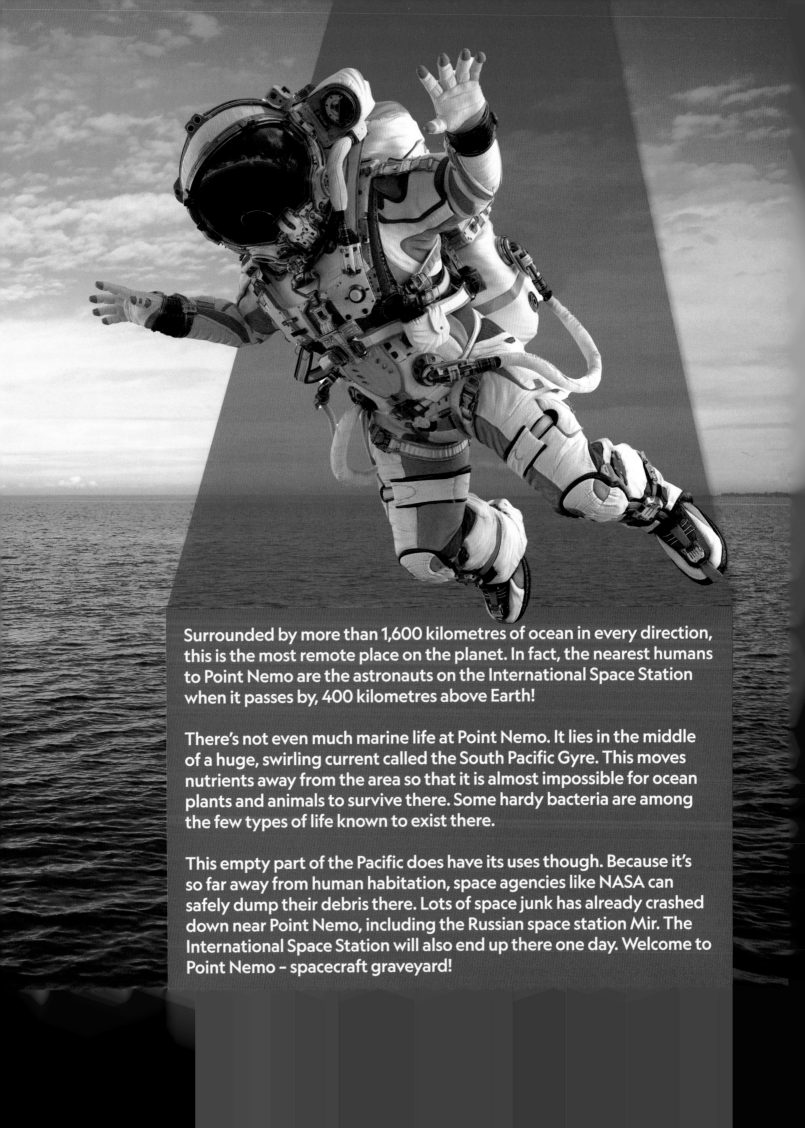

Surrounded by more than 1,600 kilometres of ocean in every direction, this is the most remote place on the planet. In fact, the nearest humans to Point Nemo are the astronauts on the International Space Station when it passes by, 400 kilometres above Earth!

There's not even much marine life at Point Nemo. It lies in the middle of a huge, swirling current called the South Pacific Gyre. This moves nutrients away from the area so that it is almost impossible for ocean plants and animals to survive there. Some hardy bacteria are among the few types of life known to exist there.

This empty part of the Pacific does have its uses though. Because it's so far away from human habitation, space agencies like NASA can safely dump their debris there. Lots of space junk has already crashed down near Point Nemo, including the Russian space station Mir. The International Space Station will also end up there one day. Welcome to Point Nemo – spacecraft graveyard!

THE ART OF erosion

Over millions of years, wind and water have carved out some unusual sculptures in the natural landscape.

CHALK STATUES

The White Desert in Egypt looks like a snowy landscape, but it gets its colour from chalk! Large chalk rock formations dot the desert like a huge sculpture park. The rocks have been shaped over centuries by wind and grinding sand.

A TREE OF STONE

High in the Siloli Desert in Bolivia stands a tree made of stone—the Árbol de Piedra. It was formed by strong, cold winds blowing grains of sand. The grains have worn away the softer rock lower down more quickly than the harder rock at the top to leave the shape of a tree.

A BASALT ELEPHANT

On the island of Heimaey in Iceland, the basalt rock left over from cooling lava has formed an unusual shape— an elephant dipping its trunk in the water. The texture of the grey rock looks just like wrinkly elephant skin, and it has even worn away in the right place to form an eye!

SANDSTONE GLOVES

The Mittens, in Monument Valley, USA, are both a type of landform called a butte. The two pillars of sandstone have been worn away in similar shapes, like a pair of mittens with their sticking-up thumbs facing each other!

A GRANITE WAVE

Wave Rock in Australia is a 14-metre-high granite cliff. The cliff face has been weathered away to form a curve that makes it look like a huge wave about to come crashing down. Rain leaves stripes down the rock, making it look even more like water.

Funky
FUNGUS FACTS

Some mushrooms
GLOW IN THE DARK.
Some scientists think mushrooms use
this 'foxfire' to attract insects, which
then spread the mushroom spores
around to help them reproduce.

You're covered in fungus! Around 200 different types of fungi live on your feet alone.

Scientists think there may be as many as **3.8 MILLION TYPES OF FUNGI** on Earth, but they estimate that more than 90 per cent of them haven't been discovered yet!

Fungi are what make **CHEESES** such as Camembert and Stilton ripen. They cause the white mould skin and the blue mould veins in these cheeses.

The **MOST POISONOUS MUSHROOM** is the death cap mushroom, *Amanita phalloides*. It causes liver failure and even death if eaten.

The prince, yellow stainer, destroying angel, jelly ear, slippery Jack, stinkhorn, grey knight and penny bun are all **TYPES OF MUSHROOMS** found in the UK.

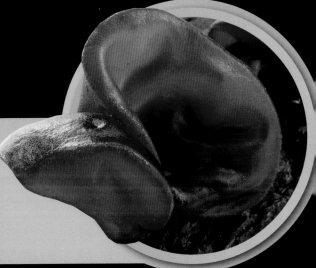

YOU'RE MORE LIKE A FUNGUS THAN YOU THINK!
Like animals – and unlike plants – fungi take in oxygen and release carbon dioxide.

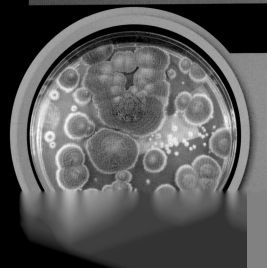

Fungi can **CAUSE INFECTIONS** such as ringworm and athlete's foot. But they can also **CURE INFECTIONS,** as some fungi produce antibiotics such as penicillin.

Mirror WORLD

Salt flats, or salt pans, are dried-up desert lakes. They form when the water in a lake evaporates, leaving behind a huge bed of sparkling salt and minerals.

The largest salt flat in the world is the Salar de Uyuni in Bolivia. Covering over 10,000 square kilometres, it's a dazzling sight! There are an estimated 10 billion tonnes of salt here, which are mined and sent all over the world. The salt you put on your dinner might even come from Salar de Uyuni! It also holds large amounts of lithium, an important chemical element. Lithium is used in all sorts of products, from medicines to mobile phones.

But there's something even more special about Salar de Uyuni. After rain, the bright, salty surface is covered with a thin layer of water. This transforms the whole area into a unique mirror world that gives a perfect reflection of the sky above. During the day, you can walk among the clouds. At sunrise and sunset the whole landscape is set ablaze. And on a clear night, you can see the stars beneath your feet!

Because the reflections are so clear, and because there are very few features on the salt flat, you can't really see the horizon. This means it's possible to create optical illusions, or 'perspective pictures' in the landscape!

19

Earth from ABOVE

From a distance, our planet resembles a blue and green marble covered by swirling white clouds. But some famous features on Earth's surface can be seen from space.

THE EYE OF THE SAHARA

Officially known as the Richat Structure, this huge dome in the western Sahara Desert measures about 40 kilometres across. It's made up of rings of different types of rock. The dome was formed from the pressure of rocks pushing up from below.

Did you KNOW?

Both human and natural lights are also visible from space. City lights and large communities of bioluminescent bacteria and algae in the oceans both shine out in the darkness.

THE PYRAMIDS OF GIZA

The biggest of the pharaohs' tombs at Giza in Egypt isn't called the 'Great' Pyramid for nothing. Each side is 230 metres at its base—about two football pitches long. And it's as high as 30 double decker buses stacked on top of each other!

THE ALMERÍA GREENHOUSES

Nearly 400 square kilometres of Almería in south-eastern Spain is covered in greenhouses! This massive glass farm produces millions of tonnes of fruit and vegetables every year. The glistening greenhouses can be spotted from space.

THE GRAND CANYON

It's 1.6 kilometres deep, 446 kilometres long and 29 kilometres wide in some places. So, it's no surprise that this giant rift in the earth in Arizona, USA, can be seen from space! The canyon was formed by the Colorado River wearing away the rock. The river itself can be seen in photographs from space.

THE GREAT BARRIER REEF

In the ocean off the north-east coast of Australia lies one of the wonders of the natural world—the Great Barrier Reef. From space, you can easily see that it's lots of separate reefs, forming amazing patterns for more than 2,000 kilometres.

Making a SPLASH...

drench yourself in some rapid rain facts!

PHANTOM RAIN
falls from the sky but evaporates before it hits the ground, so, not all rain will get you wet! This often happens in deserts.

The place with the **LOWEST RAINFALL** on Earth must be a desert, right? Well, it is – but it's a cold desert, not a hot one. The Dry Valleys in Antarctica have had very little rainfall in the last two million years – perhaps none at all!

RAINDROPS AREN'T DROP-SHAPED.
They start off as spheres, but as rain falls, air resistance 'flattens' the bottom of the drops so they're actually shaped more like jellybeans!

RAIN REALLY DOES HAVE A SMELL!

It's called 'petrichor' and it's caused by the molecule geosmin, which is created by bacteria in soil. Geosmin gets trapped in air pockets and then released into the air as rain falls, spreading the smell of rain.

FOSSILS OF RAINDROPS have been found around the world that scientists believe are billions of years old! They reveal what the early atmosphere was like on Earth.

The **LONGEST PERIOD OF RAINFALL** ever recorded was at Maunawili Ranch, on the island of Oahu in Hawaii. It rained for 331 DAYS STRAIGHT in 1939–40.

HOW FAST RAIN FALLS

depends on how big the drops are. The biggest raindrops are usually about 5 millimetres across. At that size, it can reach speeds of about 32 kilometres an hour.

COOL CAVES

MARBLE CAVES, PATAGONIA

These marble caves are white, but the water that flows through them reflects off the cave walls and ceiling and turns them an amazing turquoise colour! The water has carved out lots of arches in the rock, making the caves look like an underground cathedral.

SON DOONG CAVE, VIETNAM

The Son Doong cave is the largest cave in the world. It's high enough to fit a 40-storey building and contains a huge 'flowstone' wall—minerals deposited by water, like stalactites are—nicknamed the 'Great Wall of Vietnam'. The cave is so huge that it has its own weather system. Amazingly, it remained undiscovered until a man searching for a valuable type of wood in the forest stumbled across the cave's entrance in 1991.

ANTELOPE CANYON, USA

Wind and water erosion have carved out an incredible cave-like canyon in Arizona, USA. The sandstone was worn away by flash flooding, which created long passages with smooth, high walls. The canyon is named after the herds of pronghorn antelope that once roamed there.

BRACKEN CAVE, USA

What's a cave without bats? To see the biggest bat colony in the world, head to Bracken Cave in Texas, USA. Every year, millions of female Mexican free-tailed bats head to the cave, where they give birth in late June. They have one baby each, doubling the population of the already-crowded cave!

VATNAJÖKULL GLACIER CAVE, ICELAND

Melting ice can form caves inside glaciers. There are several ice caves in the Vatnajökull Glacier in Iceland—Europe's largest ice cap. The glacier is more than a thousand years old, but because the ice melts and refreezes, the caves are constantly changing.

Totally WEIRD!

In the Waitomo caves in New Zealand, long glowing strands hang eerily from the cave ceilings. They're created by tiny glow worms to attract prey.

Hit the OCEAN ROAD

LONDON ARCH

LOCH ARD GORGE

12 APOSTLES

The **GREAT OCEAN ROAD** runs along nearly 240 kilometres of the coast of south-east Australia, taking you on a journey through some of the country's most dramatic scenery...

First stop, **BELLS BEACH.** Surfers from all over the world come here to take on the challenge of waves that can reach more than 15 metres—three times the height of a house!

Further west along the route stands the **SPLIT POINT LIGHTHOUSE.** This part of the coast is nicknamed Shipwreck Coast because strong winds whip up the seas, causing ships to crash into underwater rocks. There are said to be about 700 wrecks here, although not all of them have been found.

There is a healthy population of koalas in the eucalyptus woodlands along the **KENNETT RIVER.**

The most famous features along the Great Ocean Road are the **12 APOSTLES —** huge limestone stacks in the shallow coastal waters. The rock they are formed of is over 20 million years old. A careful counter might notice that, despite the name, there are only eight stacks here! The other four have been eroded away by the sea.

Just around the corner lies the beach and cliffs of **LOCH ARD GORGE,** named after a ship that ran aground here in 1878. A young man named Tom Pearce was washed into the gorge. He heard a woman crying for help in the water, so swam back to rescue her. Tom and Eva were the only two survivors.

The nearby **LONDON ARCH** used to be part of a feature nicknamed London Bridge. It was a bridge of land that joined a sea arch to the mainland. But part of the cliff structure collapsed in 1990, leaving the arch stranded in the ocean.

BELLS BEACH

GREAT OCEAN ROAD

SPLIT POINT
LIGHTHOUSE

KENNETT RIVER

Did you KNOW?

Koalas are often referred to
as 'koala bears'; however,
they are actually marsupials –
so not a member of the bear
family at all!

All about the Andes...

The **ANDEAN CONDOR** is one of the world's largest flying birds. Its wingspan measures up to 3 metres.

The Andes Mountains are home to the world's highest active volcano, **COTOPAXI**, which last erupted in 2015.

Aconcagua is the highest peak in the Andes; standing 6,962 metres tall.

PURPLE CORN – called 'maiz morado' – has been grown in the Andes for thousands of years. It's kernels are dark purple and not yellow.

There are several unique animals that inhabit this mountainous region. They include the Andean mountain cat and VICUÑAS – a type of camel.

Step back in time

The **MIGHTY COLOSSEUM** in Rome, Italy, is most famous for the **GLADIATOR FIGHTS** that took place there in **ANCIENT TIMES.** But these weren't the only spectacles that ordinary **ROMANS** could enjoy in the Colosseum. The Romans may even have **FLOODED** the Colosseum and staged a **SEA BATTLE** there!

CHAPTER 2

Roam through pages 36–37 and decide if you'd like to live in ancient Rome.

From Prince to KING

On 8 September 2022, Queen Elizabeth II died, and her eldest son became King Charles III. He was 73 – the oldest person ever to inherit the British throne. Here are some other things you may not know about Britain's new monarch...

Charles became heir to the throne when he was just **THREE YEARS OLD,** when his grandfather died, and his mother became Queen. He is the **LONGEST-SERVING HEIR IN HISTORY,** waiting 70 years to wear the crown!

Totally WEIRD!

King Charles is said to be a distant descendant of the real-life Dracula, the Romanian lord known as Vlad the Impaler! The link comes through his great-grandmother, Mary of Teck.

There hasn't been a King Charles in Britain since the seventeenth century. **CHARLES I** was overthrown and beheaded in 1649. England had no monarch for 11 years before his son Charles II was restored to the throne in 1660.

The King is a history fan! He studied history for his degree from **CAMBRIDGE UNIVERSITY.** He is the first British monarch to have been to university. He also loves **ART** and **MUSIC.** The King enjoys **PAINTING** watercolours and can play three musical instruments – cello, piano and trumpet.

Charles was made **PRINCE OF WALES** when he was nine. He speaks some Welsh and is also said to be able to speak French and German well, and some Scottish Gaelic.

Charles's full name is **CHARLES PHILIP ARTHUR GEORGE.** Some people thought he might choose to be George VII to honour his grandfather (George VI) and great-grandfather (George V). Now Charles's grandson Prince George is in line to become George VII instead.

The King served in both the **ROYAL AIR FORCE** and the **ROYAL NAVY,** where he qualified as a scuba diver. He also qualified to **FLY JETS** and **HELICOPTERS.** As King, he is commander-in-chief of all the armed forces in the UK.

A question of SPORT

THE BIRTH OF BADMINTON

The game **BATTLEDORE AND SHUTTLECOCK** can be traced back to ancient Greece. Players used small bats called paddles to hit a shuttlecock back and forth without letting it hit the ground. In the 1860s, British Army officers in India added nets between the players and larger racquets were adopted —and it became known as **BADMINTON**.

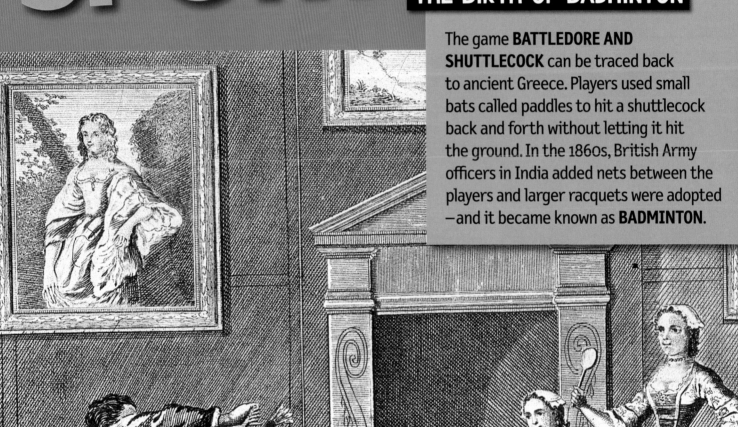

TWO BASKETS AND A BALL

BASKETBALL is one of the few sports to have been invented instead of evolving over time. In 1891, James Naismith, a PE teacher in Springfield, Massachusetts in the USA, wanted an indoor sport for the winter. He rigged up a peach basket on the rail of the balcony at each end of the gym and, using a soccer ball, invented a game where teams had to get the ball in the basket.

ARMY GAMES

POLO is a really ancient sport. In Persia in around the sixth century BCE, armies on horseback would hit a ball with sticks as a training exercise. The games would be fiercely fought, like small-scale battles!

CHILD'S PLAY

Perhaps a thousand years ago children started playing a form of **CRICKET** in England. They bowled a stone ball towards a tree stump, and their opponent used a tree branch or farm tool as a bat. Adults started playing in the 1600s. The rules varied until the 1700s when the laws of cricket were written.

RUN WITH IT!

WILLIAM WEBB ELLIS
1806 - 1872

Legend tells that in 1823, during a football match at Rugby School in England, a player named **WILLIAM WEBB ELLIS** caught the ball and started running down the field with it towards the goal. And so, the new sport of **RUGBY** was born. The men's Rugby World Cup trophy is still known as the Webb Ellis Cup, though the facts behind the legend are disputed.

Did you KNOW?

Shuttlecocks were originally known as 'birdies'. They were made of cork pierced with 16 goose feathers!

Who wants to be a Roman?

Only Roman citizens wore **TOGAS.** Enslaved people and foreigners weren't allowed to. But they probably didn't want to anyway – togas were hot, heavy and expensive!

Totally WEIRD!

Some ancient Romans drank the **BLOOD OF GLADIATORS,** which was said to cure epilepsy.

Despite popular myth, **VOMITORIUMS** weren't rooms where ancient Romans went to throw up. They were passages in amphitheatres through which spectators 'spewed' into their seats!

CHARIOT RACING was a much more popular spectator sport than **GLADIATOR FIGHTS.** The Colosseum could only hold 50,000 people, but it is thought that as many as 150,000 could fill the Circus Maximus to watch a chariot race.

A colour called **TYRIAN PURPLE** was reserved for royalty. The purple dye used to colour the emperor's clothes was made from sea snails and was very expensive!

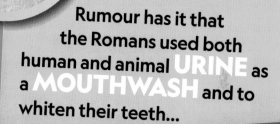

Rumour has it that the Romans used both human and animal **URINE** as a **MOUTHWASH** and to whiten their teeth...

... whether or not that's true, we do know that Romans **COLLECTED PEE** from public toilets and **SOLD IT** as a cleaning product. There was even a tax on urine!

Going to the loo was a sociable pastime in ancient Rome. **PUBLIC TOILETS** were made up of long benches with holes to poo through while enjoying a chat at the same time...

... when they'd finished, they wiped their bum with a piece of natural sponge on a stick, called a *TERSORIUM*. These were for people to share and were cleaned with vinegar or saltwater.

MEET THE
BOG PEOPLE

There are secrets buried in the bogs of northern Europe – HUMAN BODIES that have been WELL PRESERVED, some for thousands of years.

Normally, **HUMAN REMAINS** decay as time passes, leaving just the bones. But peat bogs are cold and contain very little oxygen. They are also very acidic, so they preserve bodies a bit like vinegar preserves food. Skin, hair and clothes have often survived on bog bodies. These amazing archaeological finds have revealed a lot about prehistoric people.

No one knows for sure why the bodies would have been left in the bogs. Some people think they may have been dumping grounds for the bodies of criminals or social outcasts.

The **OLDEST** bog body was found in Denmark in 1941. Scientists named the body 'Koelbjerg Woman', until DNA testing in 2016 showed that it was actually a man. He died an incredible 10,000 years ago.

TOLLUND MAN is one of the most famous bog bodies. He was so well-preserved that scientists could tell that he ate fish and porridge made of barley as his last meal. At around 2,500 years old, Tollund Man's thumbprint is also the oldest that the Danish police have on record!

In 1938, a Danish farmer discovered the body of a woman in a bog, only a few metres away from where Tollund Man was discovered a few years later. The **ELLING WOMAN'S** hair was styled in a long, elaborate plait tied into a knot at the neck, showing us what hairstyles people wore in the Iron Age!

Most bog bodies have red hair, but most of them probably didn't when they were alive. The colour is a result of the hair reacting with the acid in the bog.

Air ACES

A THRILLING RIDE

AMELIA EARHART set lots of flying records, including being the first woman to fly solo across the Atlantic. She was a thrill-seeker from an early age—as a child she helped to build a rollercoaster out of box crates in the garden. After experiencing the 2.5-metre drop she declared it was 'just like flying'!

Did you KNOW?

Amelia Earhart disappeared in 1937 while attempting to fly around the world. Neither her plane nor her body were ever found. No one knows what happened to her.

AERIAL ACROBATICS

BESSIE COLEMAN, the first Black woman to get a pilot's licence, was a stunt flyer; she amazed crowds with her tricks, such as loop-the-loops and barrel rolls. She would even walk out on the plane's wings, earning her the nickname 'Brave Bessie'.

THE RED BARON'S TREASURE

German pilot **MANFRED VON RICHTHOFEN,** aka the Red Baron, was the most feared air ace of the First World War. After each victory he would order a silver cup, which he engraved with the date. He had to stop after 60 successes because there was a shortage of silver in Germany!

A BIRD'S EYE VIEW

CHARLES LINDBERGH is one of the most famous pilots in history, but he was also a conservation campaigner. He said that his travels had made him realise how badly modern life was impacting the natural world, and that he would 'rather have birds than airplanes'.

GOING SUPERSONIC

CHARLES 'CHUCK' YEAGER became the first pilot to break the sound barrier, in October 1947. He was flying a Bell X-1 rocket-powered plane, which he'd nicknamed 'Glamorous Glennis' after his wife!

Evolution of MUSIC

NOWADAYS YOU CAN LISTEN TO MUSIC AT THE CLICK OF A BUTTON, BUT IT WASN'T ALWAYS THAT WAY...

Before humans had the ability to record sound, the only way to listen to music was if someone **PERFORMED LIVE.**

The **FIRST RECORDING** of someone singing was Édouard-Léon Scott de Martinville in 1860. He performed 'Au clair de la lune'.

PHONOGRAPHS were popular in the early 20th century. These odd-looking machines play music from records. A handle on the side of a phonograph has to be cranked to allow music to be played.

The invention of the **TRANSISTOR RADIO** in the 1950s meant people could listen to music on the move.

CASSETTE TAPES were invented in the 1960s. Music came pre-recorded on tapes or they were sold blank. This allowed people to record their own collection of songs onto their cassette. This was known as a 'mix tape'.

In 1979, the first portable cassette player was sold. People were able to insert headphones to listen to their favourite audio whenever and wherever they wanted.

COMPACT DISCS (CDs) were popular in the 80s and 90s. CDs are smaller than traditional records but can store more songs.

Digital music files called **MP3s** became popular in the 1990s. These files can be stored directly on computers and portable music devices.

STREAMING SERVICES, such as Spotify and Apple music, are how most music is listened to today. People no longer have to own physical copies of music. Instead a subscription is paid to access millions of songs by millions of artists from around the world.

Incredible creatures

Some types of snake, including VIPERS, PYTHONS and BOAS, have two types of 'sight'. They can see visible light, like other animals, but they also have holes on their face called PIT ORGANS, which detect INFRARED radiation from nearby creatures, which allows the snake to build a picture of POTENTIAL PREY!

Peer at page 52 to find out more about amazing animal eyesight.

Penguin Pals

WHAT DO YOU CALL THEM?

Most creatures have just one collective noun—the name for a group of animals. But with penguins it depends where they are and what they're doing! If they're standing around on land, they're known as a **HUDDLE.** If they're taking a walk, it's a **WADDLE.** A group of swimming penguins is a **RAFT!**

Totally WEIRD!

Male gentoo and Adélie penguins give female penguins rocks as presents when they want to mate with them!

LITTLE AND LARGE

The **SMALLEST** penguin species is the **LITTLE BLUE.** These teeny penguins from Australia and New Zealand only reach about 35 centimetres. Next to the little blue penguins, the **LARGEST** species, **EMPEROR PENGUINS,** are giants! They live in Antarctica and can reach 115 centimetres tall—about the same height as a six-year-old.

CHATTY BIRDS

A study of the calls and songs of jackass penguins suggest that the way they **COMMUNICATE** with each other follows some of the same rules and patterns as human speech! The 'words' they used most often were shorter, like our most common words. Longer calls are made up of several shorter 'syllables'.

ROCKY HOMES

Adélie and gentoo penguins don't build their **NESTS** from nice, soft, warm materials, but from pebbles and rocks. They draw a line in the ground to mark out where they're going to build, then they pile up the pebbles. These strong walls protect the eggs from damage, predators and dangers such as melting snow.

CLEVER CAMOUFLAGE

Penguins' black and white colouring is actually a type of **CAMOUFLAGE** called **COUNTERSHADING.** From above, their black backs merge with the dark ocean. From below, their white bellies blend with the light-filled water near the surface. This makes them less visible to predators.

TENNIS BALLS
turned into tiny homes

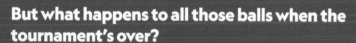

Every **JULY,** the best **TENNIS** players in the world meet at **WIMBLEDON** in **LONDON** to battle it out in the most famous tennis **CHAMPIONSHIP** in the world. The men's and women's **TOURNAMENTS** each start with **128 COMPETITORS,** who play on 18 different **COURTS** and who, over the course of the two-week tournament use a staggering **55,000 TENNIS BALLS!**

But what happens to all those balls when the tournament's over?

Some of them are sold as souvenirs, and the money is donated to charity. However, perhaps one of the quirkiest uses for the used balls has been as homes for mice!

Harvest mice live in rough grassland, crop fields and reed beds across the UK. These tiny mice build nests for themselves off the ground, out of grass and reeds. But in recent years their habitat has come under threat. This is mainly due to changes in farming methods and developments, but also because floods have washed away their nests.

Conservation groups realised that an old tennis ball was the perfect size for a harvest mouse house. They started collecting old balls and cutting holes in them, big enough for a harvest mouse but too small for predators like weasels to get in. The balls were attached to poles around 1 metre high which were stuck in the ground or attached to low branches of shrubs. The tennis balls make a safe and cosy home for the mice to build their nests and have their babies.

Did you KNOW?

Harvest mice pups are so tiny that as many as ten could fit in a single tennis ball!

A sixth sense?

Do animals have super senses? See if you can work out which of these are superstitions and which are weird but true.

SHARKS know when a hurricane is coming.
Extreme weather like hurricanes causes changes to air pressure, which marine animals can sense. Some sharks have been recorded moving to deeper water before big storms, where the water stays calmer and safer.
Verdict: **TRUE**

If **COWS** are lying down in the fields, it means rain is on the way.
Researchers tested this by putting devices on cows to measure when they stood up and when they lay down. They found that cows prefer to stand when it's hot and are simply more likely to lie down whenever the weather is cooler, including before it starts to rain. Verdict: **FALSE**

ELEPHANTS can detect earthquakes.

Elephants' feet are very sensitive to ground vibrations, which may mean they can detect shockwaves deep underground, even over long distances. In fact, elephants may use vibrations in the earth when communicating with each other. Verdict: **TRUE**

DOGS can smell fear.

A dog's sense of smell is more than 1,000 times stronger than a human's, so it knows when you start sweating! That alone wouldn't tell it you were afraid, but dogs are also super sensitive to body language, so it also knows when you tense up in fear. Verdict: **TRUE**

GOATS know when a volcano is about to erupt.

A herd of goats that lives on the slopes of the volcano Mount Etna in Italy starts behaving strangely a few hours before a large eruption happens. Scientists think they may be able to smell gases and magma rising below ground. Verdict: **TRUE**

GROUNDHOGS know when spring is coming.

On Groundhog Day, 2 February, a groundhog is coaxed out of its burrow. If it sees its shadow and scurries back in its burrow, it is said that there will be another six weeks of winter. However, statistics show that the groundhogs are more often wrong than right in their predictions! Verdict: **FALSE**

All in the EYES

HAMSTERS blink one eye at a time. They evolved this ability so they'd always have one eye out for predators!

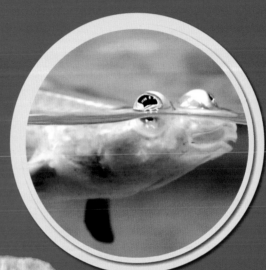

The unusual FOUR-EYED FISH can see both above and below the surface of the water at the same time!

OWLS can't move their eyeballs in their eye sockets so they have to look straight forward. Fortunately, they can turn their heads up to 270 degrees!

Because a HORSE'S eyes are on the side of its head, it can see almost all the way around. It has just two blind spots – directly behind it and right in front of its nose!

CATS' eyes 'glow in the dark' because of a mirror-like structure on the retina. This reflects light back into their eyes and boosts their night vision.

BUMBLEBEES have compound eyes, each with up to 6,000 lenses, or facets. These amazing eyes allow the bees to identify colour faster than any other creature – and five times faster than humans!

DOLPHINS have to keep half their brain conscious when they sleep so they don't stop breathing. That means they sleep with one eye open! The left eye closes when the right part of the brain sleeps and vice versa.

An OSTRICH'S eye is around 5 centimetres across, which make it bigger than this big bird's brain!

Totally WEIRD!

Photoreceptors are the cells that allow animals to see. You have three types of photoreceptors, which mean you see red, blue and green. The MANTIS SHRIMP has up to 16. The shrimp have very small brains though, so scientists don't know what they do with such advanced eyesight!

FAT BEAR
Week

Katmai National Park in Alaska, USA, is home to some of the biggest brown bears in the world. They live around Brooks River, where they feast on salmon from the river and berries and roots on land. Every year, as autumn approaches, the bears start to fatten up to help them survive the long winter in hibernation.

Some of the already huge bears put on a lot of weight! So much so that the bears of Brooks River have become the stars of a week-long championship held online every year known as **FAT BEAR WEEK!**

Pictures of the bears are posted on the explore.org website, showing them before and after they fatten up for winter. There are even biographies telling people about the bears' looks, personality and fishing skills!

The public vote between sets of two matched-up bears to choose the one they think has gained the most weight. The winner of each pair goes through to the next round, and the public chooses again between new matches. Bears are knocked out until finally the Fattest Bear is chosen!

More than one million people voted in the 2022 championship but Bear 747 was almost cheated out of the crown due to voter fraud! Organisers noticed a sudden rush of votes in his match-up with Bear 435, which they realised were all from fake email addresses. Luckily, they fixed the fraud and Bear 747 was able to take his rightful place as the winner.

In a warm-up competition, Fat Bear Junior, people vote for the cuddliest cub! The winner goes through to the main competition, where they go up against the full-grown bears.

Did you **KNOW?**

The most titles in Fat Bear Week have gone to Bear 480, known as Otis, who has won the competition four times.

The winner of the 2022 competition was Bear 747. This beast of a bear is estimated to weigh a whopping 635 kilograms (about half the weight of an average car) and may be largest bear in the world.

Are you talking to ME?

Sometimes animals communicate with each other in the weirdest ways...

GORILLAS HUM

Do you sometimes hum a little tune to yourself as you get ready for dinner? If so, you'd get on well with a gorilla! The big males known as **SILVERBACKS** have been heard **HUMMING** around mealtimes. This might be a way of letting their family know that food is ready, and a way of saying 'don't disturb me' while they're eating.

DHOLES are a type of wild dog. They usually live in packs of up to 12 but they sometimes form super-packs with over 30 members. If a pack is spread out over a wide area, these dogs don't bark to stay in touch—they **WHISTLE!** The sounds are so distinctive that you can identify a particular dhole by its 'voice.'

SPERM WHALES CLICK

You've probably heard of whales singing, but have you heard of them **CLICKING?** SPERMS WHALES use this unusual sound to send information across huge distances in the water. Each series of clicks is called a coda. The sound is so loud that if you were underwater nearby it would burst your eardrums.

DHOLES WHISTLE

RHINOS LEAVE A (SMELLY) NOTE

There's no toilet privacy for **WHITE RHINOS.** They use communal loos and pass messages in their poo. By taking a good sniff of **DUNG,** a rhino can find out everything it needs to know about the rhino that left the deposit—whether it's male or female, how old it is, whether it's healthy or ill, and whether a female is ready to mate!

Did you KNOW?

Ravens use a form of sign language to get across certain messages. They use their wings and beaks to send signs to other ravens.

Creatures
of the night

SNEAKY SNAKES

EYELASH VIPERS live in trees and wake at night to catch their prey. They get their name from the scales above their eyes, which look a bit like eyelashes. They help camouflage the creature by breaking up its shape against the tree branches.

Did you KNOW?

Nocturnal animals often have features that help them move quietly. For example, owls have special feather linings that muffle the sound of their wings, and four-legged animals have footpads that help them sneak around silently.

SPINES IN THE DARK

SPINY MICE get their name from their stiff, spiky hairs that work in the same way as a hedgehog's spines. These night-time creatures may be small, but they have an amazing ability—if they are injured, they heal without any scars on their body.

BIG BATS

Despite their name, **FLYING FOXES** are actually bats—one of the largest bat species in the world. But flying foxes don't use echolocation to find their way in the dark. Instead, they have brilliant eyesight and a sharp sense of smell that helps them find berries for breakfast!

TOADS ON THE ROAD

ROCOCO TOADS are one of the biggest wild toads in the world, growing to about the size of an electronic tablet. They like dark, damp conditions so will often take a walk on a rainy night.

CAN YOU SPOT ME?

SMALL-SPOTTED GENETS aren't true cats, although they look a lot like them. Their long, flexible bodies mean they can squeeze through small gaps—if a genet can get its head through a hole, its body will follow!

OWL MONKEYS

Like many nocturnal animals, **NIGHT MONKEYS** have big eyes, designed to capture as much light as possible in the gloom. Their eyes are what earned them their other name, owl monkeys. These monkeys prefer to be active after dark.

ELEPHANT MINERS
of Mount Elgon

When you think of **ELEPHANTS,** you probably picture them roaming sunny grasslands. It's true that most elephants live an outdoor life, where there's plenty of space and sunshine. But one herd of elephants in Africa has chosen a less typical lifestyle.

MOUNT ELGON stands on the border between Kenya and Uganda. There, salt water has worn caves into the rock, and these have become a favourite place for the Mount Elgon elephants. The elephants' regular plant diet isn't rich in minerals such as salt, so they must find them elsewhere. In Kitum Cave, they use their tusks to chip away at the salty rock, then eat the tiny fragments.

MOUNT ELGON

Elephants often return to **FEED AND DRINK** in the same places. They even pass down information in the herd from one generation to the next. Over many years, the changing herd of elephants at Mount Elgon has made quite a dent in the caves! The herd is known to venture as far as 150 metres into the darkness to mine the salt there.

These unusual elephants are under threat. They sometimes damage farmers' crops, which puts them in conflict with local communities. **THE MOUNT ELGON ELEPHANT PROJECT** was launched in 2017 to protect the cave elephants. One of the ways they do this is by tracking the animals so they know when they're getting near farmland and can head them off before they do any damage!

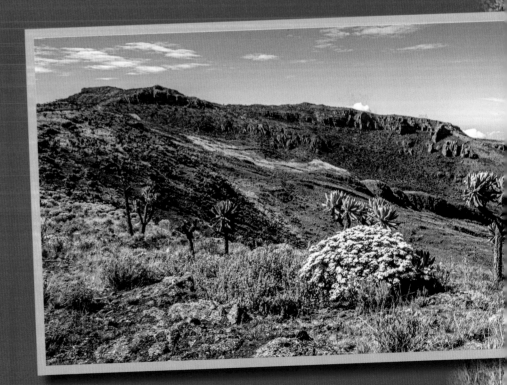

Whose POO?

Because **ELEPHANTS** eat a lot of plants, their dung is high in fibre. Because of this, in parts of Asia, elephant poo is picked up, pulped and made into paper!

SLOTHS do everything slowly, including going to the loo! Just once a week a sloth comes down from its tree to poo, in what's been nicknamed 'the poo dance'.

Totally WEIRD!

Penguin poo (or guano as bird poop is officially known) contains nitrous oxide – otherwise known as laughing gas. On one occasion, some researchers studying penguins in Antarctica were exposed to so much of it that it made them start behaving strangely!

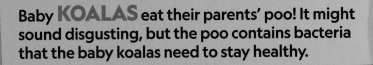

Baby **KOALAS** eat their parents' poo! It might sound disgusting, but the poo contains bacteria that the baby koalas need to stay healthy.

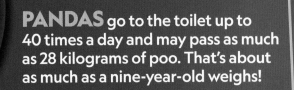

PANDAS go to the toilet up to 40 times a day and may pass as much as 28 kilograms of poo. That's about as much as a nine-year-old weighs!

SPERM WHALES produce a substance in their intestines called ambergris, which is so valuable that it's nicknamed 'floating gold'. This form of whale poo can be used to make perfume!

VULTURES have an unusual way of chilling out – they poo on their own legs! As the water in the faeces evaporates, the blood vessels in the legs and feet cool down.

LLAMA poo is helping the environment! Llama droppings are being used to treat water that has been polluted by mining. The poop helps remove high levels of acid from the water.

Peculiar POOCHES

BLOODHOUNDS
have the most scent receptors of any dog breed. They have such a powerful sense of smell that they can detect smells that are over 12 days old.

POODLES – the
national dog of France – originated in Germany. The name poodle derives from the German term 'pudel' which means 'to splash'. In France, their name translates to 'duck dog'.

CHOW CHOWS are born
with a pink tongue, but by the time they are six months old it has changed to a blue-black colour!

NEAPOLITAN MASTIFFS look cute with their wrinkly faces, but this Italian dog breed was used by Roman soldiers when they went into battle.

CHIHUAHUAS are the world's smallest dog breed and are also one of the oldest. Old folklore suggested that chihuahuas had the power to cure asthma by taking the condition from their owner, although there is no medical evidence to support this.

DALMATIANS are born with a gene that cause many of them to struggle with their hearing. Around 20% of dalmatians have some level of deafness.

BASENJIS don't bark. Instead, they make a yodelling sound.

A GREYHOUND would beat a cheetah in a long distance race. Although cheetahs are fast over short distances, greyhounds can maintain there high speed for longer.

BRILLIANT
BODY PARTS

EMPEROR TAMARINS have long whiskers that look like a **HUGE MOUSTACHE.** These monkeys are believed to be named after German emperor Wilhelm II who also had a large moustache.

Did you **KNOW?**

Emperor tamarins are amazing acrobats. They can jump up to 9 metres through trees and use their their tails to balance as they make their way through the canopy.

TOUCANS can be found zipping through the rainforests of Central and South America and are renowned for their long, bright and **CURVED BEAKS.**

These brilliant beaks aren't just for show – they are useful for finding food. Toucans use them to get to fruit that otherwise would be out of reach and to pick insects out of tree bark.

CATERPILLARS are extremely flexible. Their bodies are made up of lots of **SEGMENTS** and each of these parts have their own set of muscles. This structure allows these minibeasts to stretch, bend and twist.

Did you KNOW?

Okapis make an unusual sound when they're communicating with each other. The low-pitched noise sounds a bit like a deep, rumbling cough. Scientists call it a 'bleat-roar' because it's a mix between a bleat (from a sheep) and a roar (from a lion)!

OKAPIS are related to giraffes! Even though they look different, they share some characteristics such as long necks and **PURPLE TONGUES.**

Okapis also have a unique smell. **SPECIAL GLANDS** on their feet produce a strong scent that they use to mark their territory. Some people think it smells like old socks!

Super science and technology

The **LARGEST GOLD COIN** ever was made in Australia in 2011. It **MEASURES** 80 centimetres across and 12 centimetres deep and is worth about **£50 MILLION**. It's known as the 'one-tonne kangaroo' because the coin weighs a **SOLID TONNE** and pictures a **RED KANGAROO** on one side!

CHAPTER 4

NGAROO 1 TONNE 9999 GOLD

RED KANGAROO

P

A 2012

Mine your way over to page 76 for more amazing information about gold.

Particle PARTY

COSMIC MUONS ▶

Earth is under constant bombardment from **MUONS**. These particles are created when cosmic rays from outer space hit Earth's atmosphere and collide with the particles there. Muons are born and die in a split second – actually 2.2 microseconds – but they travel so fast that they can penetrate Earth's surface.

Totally WEIRD!

For almost 50 years, scientists believed that a particular type of boson particle existed. The problem was, they couldn't prove it. It was only in 2013, thanks to experiments in a huge particle accelerator, that the theory of what became known as the Higgs Boson was finally proven.

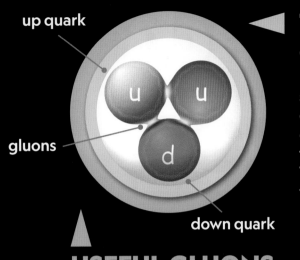

up quark

gluons

down quark

TASTY QUARKS

QUARKS come in different **FLAVOURS!** But they're not sweet or salty. The flavours of quarks are up, down, strange, charm, bottom and top! These teeny particles are very old. They formed one picosecond – that's one trillionth of a second – after the Big Bang.

USEFUL GLUONS

The clue to what the particles called **GLUONS** do is in the name. Yes, it really does mean *glue* + *on*. These force-carrying particles JOIN TOGETHER quarks to make bigger particles. It takes a lot of energy to break up gluons and quarks – temperatures of around 2 *trillion* degrees!

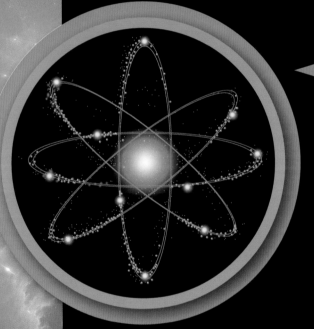

TEENY ELECTRONS

You probably know about **ELECTRONS**. They're the negatively charged particles that move around in atoms. But do you know how small they are? Well, they're unimaginably small. So small, in fact, that scientists don't actually know how small they are, because they can't find the edges of an electron to measure it!

BRIGHT PHOTONS ▶

There are more **PHOTONS** in the universe than any other particle. That's a good thing because photons are particles of light. Photons are being created and destroyed all the time. For example, the light in your TV creates photons, which travel to your eyes, where they're absorbed and destroyed. Weirdly, photons behave like waves, as well as particles!

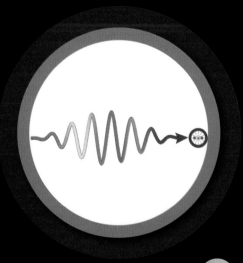

Cockroach CYBORGS

Cockroaches are known for their **SURVIVAL SKILLS.** It's not totally true that they could survive a nuclear blast, but they can definitely cope with much higher doses of radiation than humans. They can eat almost anything but can also go a long time without food or water. They also have the amazing ability to withstand pressure, making them virtually impossible to crush! On top of all that, they can move quickly and can squeeze into small spaces.

All these characteristics attracted the attention of a team of Japanese scientists working on **FUTURISTIC WAYS** of dealing with disasters. When buildings collapse in an earthquake, for example, people are trapped underneath the rubble. Could cockroaches be used to locate them?

The team came up with the idea of 'CYBORG INSECTS'. These were real insects rigged up with electronic 'backpacks' that would allow them to be controlled remotely. They chose the Madagascar hissing cockroach because it was big enough to carry the equipment and it had no wings to get in the way.

The insect's abdomen is covered with a specially designed film made of **SOLAR CELLS,** 1/25th the width of a human hair. The solar cells generate power that sends signals to the cockroach's legs, telling it where to go.

There's still work to do. The backpacks full of electronics need to be smaller, so the insects can move more easily, and the researchers want to put **TINY CAMERAS** on the insects' backs too. But who knows—sometime soon, first responders in an emergency might be a team of cockroaches!

Did you KNOW?

The Bluetooth signals that the controllers send bypass the cockroaches' brain and instruct its legs where to go. But the brain is still needed to make the insect's muscles move.

DRONING on

DANCING DRONE DISPLAY

For Queen Elizabeth II's Platinum Jubilee in 2022, 400 drones took to the skies over Buckingham Palace to perform an incredible light show. The company, SkyMagic, controlled the drones in perfect sync to create patterns and pictures in the sky, including the Union Jack flag and the Queen's favourite dog, the corgi.

TO THE RESCUE!

On Christmas Day 2021, two brothers set off for a hike in Virginia, USA. As darkness fell, they hadn't returned—they were clearly lost on the mountain. The search and recue team sent out a drone equipped with a thermal imaging camera. This tech detects heat that comes off the human body. Having located the brothers, the human rescue team could go in on foot and bring them home.

CLEANING MACHINES

Being small and able to fly means that drones can get to places that are difficult or dangerous for humans. Specially designed drones with mini mops can wash windows high up. Or they can hover with a hose to clean the outside of mucky buildings from top to bottom!

DINNER DELIVERIES

Forget take-away delivered by drivers on bikes, using pedal power to get you your dinner. The future of food deliveries is drones! Customers place an order online or by phone as usual. The food is then cooked, packed up and attached to a drone. How it's delivered varies. It could be lowered by cable to the customer's door or dropped off to a driver who takes it the rest of the way.

Totally WEIRD!

Some people have even used drones to take their dog for walks. Drones aren't equipped to clean up dog-doo yet, though!

TUTANKHAMUN'S MASK is one of the most famous gold objects ever discovered. It is made from sheets of gold, heated and hammered to form the face of the pharaoh.

Going for GOLD

We mine gold from below ground but this precious metal isn't formed in Earth's crust - it comes from **OUTER SPACE!** Gold forms when stars die in supernova explosions.

Totally WEIRD!

Because gold is so pure, in medieval times people thought that drinking melted gold mixed with crushed emeralds would cure the Plague.

The **SHIP OF GOLD** is the nickname for the *SS Central America*. The steamship sank in 1857 after being hit by a hurricane. On board were millions of dollars worth of gold nuggets and other artefacts from the California gold rush.

Gold is **PRACTICALLY INDESTRUCTIBLE,** which means that pretty much all the gold that's ever been mined on Earth is still around somewhere.

The **FIRST GOLD COINS** were made and used in Lydia (now part of Turkey) more than 2,500 years ago on the orders of the fabulously wealthy King Croesus. People still use the expression 'as rich as Croesus'!

The **CHEMICAL SYMBOL** for gold is Au, from its Latin name Aurum. It's atomic number is 79, which means there are 79 protons in its nucleus.

Olympic **GOLD MEDALS** aren't gold. In fact they only contain about 6 grams of gold. At least 92.5% of the gold medal is silver.

WEIRD WATER...
Why don't
ICEBERGS SINK?

1. Water is more dense in liquid form than it is as a solid.

2. Icebergs aren't just solid blocks of ice —they are packed with billions of air bubbles.

3. The world's seas and oceans contain lots of salt. This water is more dense than the fresh water that makes up icebergs.

WHY DO APPLES BOB?

Have you ever gone **APPLE BOBBING** on Halloween and wondered how the fruit floats instead of sinking to the bottom of the barrel? The answer is that apples are empty (sort of)! About 25% of an apple is nothing but air, which means that they're lighter than water.

HOW DOES SALT HELP FLOATABILITY?

Salt water is more dense than fresh water, so things float more easily on it. The **DEAD SEA** is an incredible 34% salt, which means that it takes no effort at all to stay afloat on its surface. The downside is that the water is so dense that it's really hard to swim in it!

Totally WEIRD!

A peeled orange sinks but an orange with its skin on floats. That seems the wrong way round, but it happens because the peel is full of tiny air pockets, which actually make the orange less dense than when it's peeled.

HOW CAN YOU TELL IF AN EGG IS FRESH?

You can tell if an **EGG** is safe to eat by putting it in a bowl of cold water. If the egg sinks, it's fresh, but if it floats, it's old and probably not too tasty! This happens because inside the egg is a small air sac, which gets bigger as the egg gets older. When the air sac gets big enough, the egg will float.

WHAT ROCK FLOATS?

It seems certain that if you chuck a rock into a pool, it'll sink like a stone. But that's not always the case. **PUMICE** is a type of rock formed when lava from volcanoes hardens. It cools so fast that loads of gas bubbles get trapped in the rock, which makes it light enough to float.

Beam me UP!

Every now and then, after dark in some of the coldest parts of the world, a strange phenomenon occurs – mysterious pillars of light can be seen stretching from the Earth high into the sky. It might look like a UFO is sending down beams ready for landing, but in fact, light pillars are an optical effect based on simple science.

When it's very cold – usually below zero degrees – tiny ice crystals form in the air. They don't sink to the ground, but instead remain suspended a little way above it. Because these ice crystals are flat, they're great reflectors.

The crystals catch light from nearby objects, such as street lamps. Together, they act as a giant mirror, reflecting the light into the sky in columns. The bigger the crystals, the more dramatic the light show! It also helps if there's no wind to disrupt the reflection.

Real beams of light are columns of light particles travelling in a particular direction, so light pillars aren't beams in a strictly scientific sense. You wouldn't be able to see the pillar if you were either above or below the light source. They're just an amazing optical illusion caused by light reflecting off ice.

Have fun in your SMART HOME

Smart gadgets have taken over our homes. Here's how to make the most of them.

Get your kitty a real **FELINE FITNESS TRACKER** and see who is fitter —you or your cat!

Ask **ALEXA** to make you a sandwich and see what she says....

ring

Avoid annoying neighbours by installing a **VIDEO DOORBELL** so you know when they come knocking (or ringing!)

Start a conversation with **SIRI** by saying 'Knock knock'.

Start your day in the right way by asking your **SMART MIRROR** what's going on in the world, or what to wear for the weather.

Morning News

07:35
TODAY

Take a screenshot of a friend's **MOBILE PHONE** home screen, set it as their background and watch as they scratch their head thinking their phone has frozen.

Set your **SMART LIGHT** to match your mood — or even link it to your smart speakers and see the colours dance in time to your music.

Spectacular Structures

The **GOLDEN GATE BRIDGE** in SAN FRANCISCO, USA, is said to be the **MOST-PHOTOGRAPHED BRIDGE** in the world.

Cross over to page 92 for more record-breaking bridges.

DUBAI – CITY OF AWESOME ARCHITECTURE

Dubai is famous as the home of the world's tallest skyscraper, the Burj Khalifa, but it has plenty of other amazing architecture too.

URBAN RAINFOREST

THE GREEN PLANET is an indoor rainforest in the heart of the city! The glass bio-dome has four levels—the Canopy at the top, the Midstory, the Forest Floor and the Flooded Rainforest.

Did you KNOW?

The city has 240 skyscrapers – buildings over 150 metres tall. Twenty-eight of them are 'supertall' skyscrapers, more than 300 metres.

TWISTED AND TURN

The twisting **CAYAN TOWER** stands on the edge of the marina in Dubai, where the wealthy bring their yachts! Each floor was designed at 1.2 degrees round from the floor below, building to a 90-degree spiral from bottom to top.

EXPLORE THE OPUS

The unusual building known as the **OPUS** looks like a kind of cube with the middle scooped out. It's two separate towers joined by an uneven three-storey bridge high above the ground. Covered in glass, the Opus reflects the other buildings all around.

FRAMING THE PAST

The giant frame that stands in **ZABEEL PARK** is one of the strangest structures in Dubai! It's actually an observatory offering amazing views over old Dubai to the north and the glistening modern structures of the newer city in the south.

THAT'S A-MAZE-ING

MAZE TOWER is the largest vertical maze in the world. It's actually a series of balconies up the 55-storey building, but the pattern isn't just for show—it's a real puzzle. At night the building comes alive with multi-coloured lights and a circular video wall at the top called the Maze Eye.

CREATING THE FUTURE

The **MUSEUM OF THE FUTURE** was designed in a torus, or ring, shape. The windows form a poem in Arabic, which includes the words: *The future belongs to those who can imagine it, design it, and execute it. It isn't something you await, but rather create.*

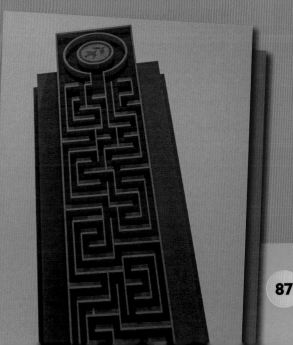

Palace of BUBBLES

The **BUBBLE PALACE** – or Palais Bulles as they call it in France – might be the strangest structure on the French Riviera!

The architect, Antti Lovag, was inspired by prehistoric cave houses when he designed the house. That works well considering its situation, set into a cliff overlooking the sea. But early human cave dwellings wouldn't have been as extensive as the Bubble Palace – or as luxurious! It has 29 rooms, including 10 bedrooms, on six levels connected with spiral staircases and curved corridors.

Outside, waterfalls cascade down the curved walls of the building. It is surrounded by tropical gardens and three swimming pools. There's even an outdoor amphitheatre that can seat 500 people.

As its name suggests, the Bubble Palace is all circles and spheres. Lovag hated straight lines! He thought they were 'an aggression against nature'. Even the beds are round to fit into the circular rooms! Round portholes in the domed ceilings let in light. The staircases are spiral, and all the corridors are curved.

Its original owner was a wealthy French businessperson. Fashion designer Pierre Cardin bought it in 1992 and many celebrities hung out there. Cardin died in 2020 and there is talk of turning this artistic building into a centre for the arts.

Totally WEIRD!

The problem with the Bubble Palace is that it's not very practical to live in! Pierre Cardin apparently never actually lived there himself. He just used it for entertaining guests, hosting parties and putting on fashions shows.

Time TELLERS

The medieval **ZIMMER TOWER** in Lier, Belgium, consists of 13 dials – a main clock face and 12 others, showing solar time, lunar time and the signs of the zodiac, among others!

The **SUN CLOCK** in Nakano, Japan, is a type of automaton clock. On the hour, bells ring and little figures appear playing musical instruments.

Did you KNOW?

Big Ben is the name of one of the bells at the Houses of Parliament in London, not the clock. The clock and the bells are housed in the Elizabeth Tower.

The **TOWER OF THE WINDS** in Athens, Greece, is more than 2,000 years old. It once housed eight sundials and a water clock, but now only the tower remains.

Standing in the middle of a roundabout in Dubai, with fountains underneath, the **DEIRA CLOCKTOWER** is said to be one of the most beautiful in the world!

At 100 metres high, the **JOSEPH CHAMBERLAIN MEMORIAL CLOCK TOWER** at Birmingham University is the tallest freestanding clock tower in the world.

At the top of the **ROYAL CLOCK TOWER** in Mecca, Saudi Arabia, are the highest – and the largest – clock faces in the world. The clocks can be seen from 17 kilometres away.

The **CHIANG RAI CLOCK TOWER** in Thailand was designed to reflect traditional Thai architecture. The golden structure comes to life every evening with a light show!

The **NEW TOWN HALL CLOCK TOWER** in Munich, Germany, is 80 metres high. Every day, a series of figures appear on the front of the tower to re-enact the wedding of the sixteenth-century Duke Wilhelm V.

Bridge RECORDS

Totally WEIRD!

The world's largest Bluetooth device is Tower Bridge in London. In 2007, the bridge was modified to be able to detect other people's phones and other Bluetooth-enabled devices and display their location in coloured pixels on the bridge.

LONGEST

The current world record-holder for the longest bridge is the **DANYANG-KUNSHAN GRAND BRIDGE** in China. The 164-kilometre bridge is part of the Jinghu High-Speed Railway. It's specially designed to stay standing even in the event of an earthquake, a typhoon or being rammed into by a big ship!

BUSIEST

The **GEORGE WASHINGTON BRIDGE** crosses the Hudson River between New York and New Jersey. When it opened in 1932 it had six lanes for traffic and carried 5.5 million vehicles. Today there are 14 lanes – seven each way on two decks – and it's crossed by more than 100 million vehicles a year, making it the world's busiest bridge.

Which of these **THREE BRIDGES** do **YOU** think would be the most **TERRIFYING** to **WALK ACROSS?**

The Canopy Walk is a series of wire rope bridges between the trees in the rainforest of Ghana. Be warned – you might share your crossing with monkeys or even snakes!

The Langkawi Sky Bridge in Malaysia feels suspended in the sky. It's 660 metres high and curved so you can't see where it ends when you set off!

The bridge over the Zhangjiajie Grand Canyon has a glass walkway, which means you can see straight through to the 300-metre drop below!

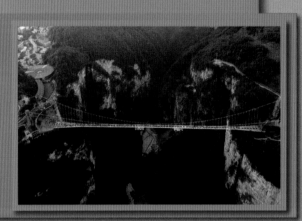

OLDEST

It's hard to know for sure which is the oldest bridge still standing, but the **ARKADIKO BRIDGE** is one of the contenders. This ancient arch bridge designed for chariots was built in Greece sometime between 1300 and 1190 BCE. Amazingly, it's still safe to cross today – on foot!

TEN on
TERMITE MOUNDS

1. Termite mounds are made from a combination of **SALIVA**, **SOIL** and **DUNG**.

2. These spectacular structures are around 2.5 metres tall but some can be over **8 METRES HIGH!**

3. The structures are very hardy and can survive for **CENTURIES**.

4. The termites that build mounds are **BLIND**. They work in the dark and use their senses of touch and smell to navigate.

5 The inside of a mound is filled with a network of COMPLEX TUNNELS and chambers used for living and storing food.

6 The SIZE and SHAPE of mounds can vary depending on the type of termite that built them. Some can be cone-shaped and others like towers.

7 The QUEEN of a termite colony can lay tens of thousands of eggs every day.

8 Some termite species build their mounds completely UNDERGROUND.

9 MOUNDOPOLIS in Brazil is an area with around 200 million mounds.

10 Moundopolis covers such a large area that is can be seen from SATELLITES in space.

Weird Wonders of the WORLD

The New Seven Wonders of the World are all super-famous structures, but there are still things you might not know about them.

THE GREAT WALL OF CHINA

A more accurate name would be the Great Walls of China. In places, it's layered into two, three or even four **DIFFERENT WALLS.**

CHICHEN-ITZA

On the equinoxes, when day and night are the same length, a **SHADOW** in the shape of a **SERPENT** crawls down the steps of the Temple of Kukulkan at Chichen-Itza.

PETRA

Archaeologists believe that only about 15% of the **ANCIENT CITY** of Petra has been explored so far. Many more structures and treasures remain to be uncovered.

CHRIST THE REDEEMER
The huge statue of Christ the Redeemer in Brazil is **STRUCK BY LIGHTNING** an average of four times a year. It would suffer more than that, but lightning rods on the structure deflect most strikes.

THE COLOSSEUM
The hundreds of small holes in the Colosseum walls are a result of **SCAVENGING** when the building first fell into disrepair. People pulled out the iron clamps originally used to hold the structure together.

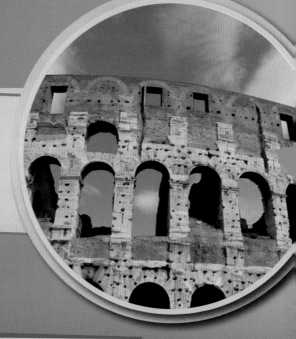

THE TAJ MAHAL
More than **1,000 ELEPHANTS**, as well as 20,000 people, were involved in building the great mausoleum the Taj Mahal.

MACHU PICCHU
The Inca city was built using a method called **ASHLAR**, which involves cutting stones so precisely that not even a piece of paper would fit between them when put together.

Get a move on

The **LONDON BOOSTER** was created to commemorate the **2012 LONDON OLYMPICS.** The double-decker was fitted with **MUSCULAR ARMS** and was able to do **PRESS-UPS!** Although it was based on an old London double-decker bus, sadly it **DIDN'T DRIVE!**

CHAPTER 6

Wheel your way over to page 104 to see some more bizarre buses.

Airlander – the future of flight?

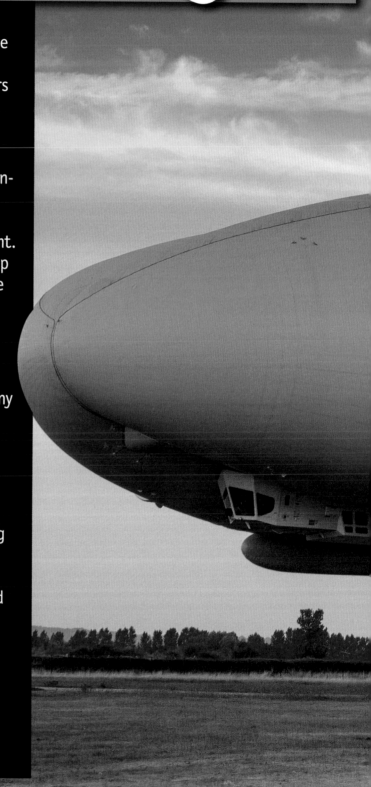

Early human-powered flight developed with hot-air balloons. But there was a problem with them—because they couldn't really be steered, you ended up going wherever the wind carried you. So, ingenious inventors began developing a different balloon-type craft that could be steered. And so, the airship was born.

In the early years of the 20th century, German Ferdinand von Zeppelin developed a series of hydrogen-fuelled airships which took his name. The Zeppelins became very famous and for a while it seemed as though they would really take off as the future of flight. But hydrogen catches fire easily and in 1937 the airship *Hindenburg* fell from the sky in a ball of flames. People stopped building airships and passenger planes took over the skies.

Fast forward 80 years and the huge problem of emissions from air travel had people once again wondering if there was a different way to fly. A company called Hybrid Air Vehicles (HAV) began building a new type of airship, powered by helium—safer than hydrogen!—and electricity.

At 92 metres, the *Airlander 10* is the longest aircraft in the world—more than 18 metres longer than the biggest passenger plane. It's made of incredibly strong carbon fibre and equipped with a set of skids, so it can take off from and land on all different terrains, including snow and even water! It's also been designed with glass floors, so that the 100 passengers on board can see the world passing by below.

In 2022, HAV received its first order from an airline company, Air Nostrum, which plans to use 10 airships to carry passengers on flights across Spain. It looks like the lessons of the past have inspired a more environmentally friendly future for flight!

The Airlander 10 has been nicknamed the 'flying bum'.

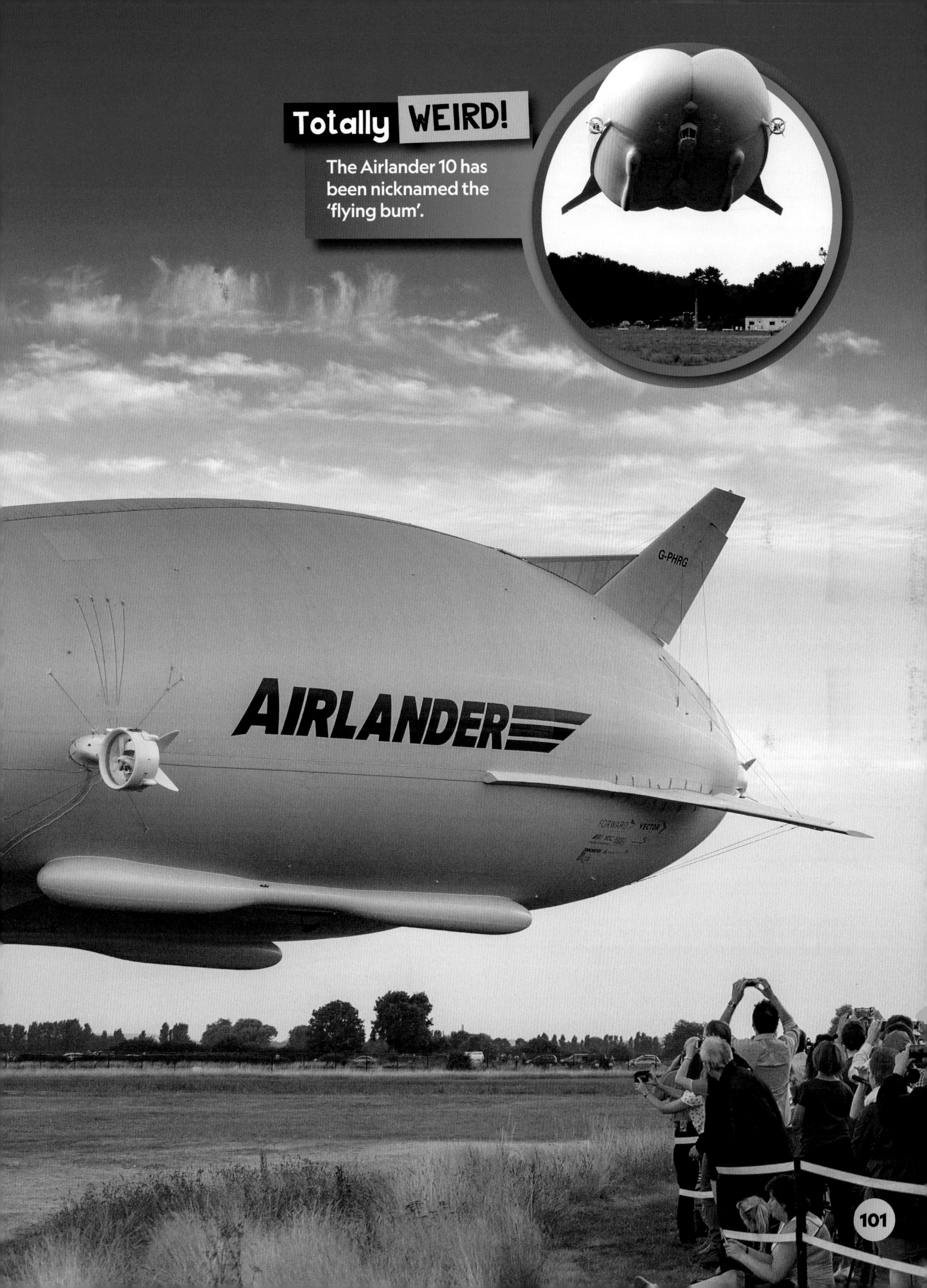

AIRLANDER

G-PHRG

TRAFFIC CHAOS

CONGESTED CITIES

In 2023, the five worst cities for traffic troubles (with the average number of hours people lose stuck in jams each year) were:
1   London (156)
2   Chicago (155)
3   Paris (138)
4   Boston (134)
5   Bogota (122)

ROUND AND ROUND AND...

The Magic Roundabout in Swindon, UK, is one of the craziest junctions anywhere in the world. It's made up of one big roundabout surrounded by five smaller ones. A lot of the car confusion comes from the fact that you drive clockwise round the outer roundabouts but anticlockwise round the middle!

THE MAGIC ROUNDABOUT

Ring road
Cirencester
A4289

(M4)

Town centre

Marlborough
Burford
Oxford

H A&E

A4312

WORLD'S WORST TRAFFIC JAM

It's bad enough getting stuck in traffic for an hour, so imagine how frustrated drivers on the Beijing-Tibet Expressway in China were when they got caught up in a 12-day traffic jam in August 2010. The tailbacks stretched for 100 kilometres!

SHARE AND SHARE ALIKE

How does Google Maps know when and where traffic is bad? It gathers data from everyone on the roads who has their location switched on in the app. It basically crowdsources the information and then helpfully shares it around!

SPAGHETTI JUNCTION

The Judge Harry Pregerson Interchange in Los Angeles, USA, is a total tangle of concrete ramps and roads! At 40 metres high, it's what's known as a 'stack interchange', which works as a junction between two highways, to keep traffic flowing. You'd just better hope you don't get on the wrong road!

Did you KNOW?

Traffic jams aren't always caused by accidents or roadworks. Sometimes all it takes is one person braking suddenly. Each car behind is then forced to brake to a greater degree. Jams like this are known as 'phantom traffic jams'.

Bizarre BUSES

GET ON A GOAT!

Colombia's CHIVAS (which translates as 'goats') are colourfully painted open-air buses. Passengers sit on wooden benches inside the bus, but if it gets full, they can always climb a ladder and sit on the roof!

POO POWER!

Bio buses are powered completely by BIOMETHANE gas, so they're very environmentally friendly. The gas comes from food waste – and human waste! The bus heads to the local sewage plant to fuel up!

CUTE COACH

In Japan, the buses that take children to pre-school are often designed to look like cute animals or favourite CARTOON CHARACTERS, such as Hello Kitty, Pikachu and Snoopy!

BUS WITH A VIEW

The **CITYRAMA** sightseeing bus was a familiar sight on the streets of Paris in the 1950s, 60s and 70s. It seated 30 passengers on the bottom and 20 on the top, who enjoyed great views through the glass and information through headphones on each seat.

IS IT A BUS? IS IT A TRAIN?

It's both! The first **DUAL-MODE VEHICLE (DMV)** was recently launched in Japan. It looks like a small bus and runs on rubber tyres on the road. When it hits the rails, steel wheels are lowered from beneath to keep it on track.

LONDON DUCKS

The London **DUCK BUS** takes tourists on an unusual journey round the capital, on the city streets and down the River Thames! The buses are actually old amphibious vehicles from the Second World War, adapted so they still safely travel on both land and water.

Totally WEIRD!

No full triple-decker buses have ever been built – except the famous purple Knight Bus from the *Harry Potter* movies. The prop bus is now at Universal Studios in Florida, USA.

Random rules of the
ROAD

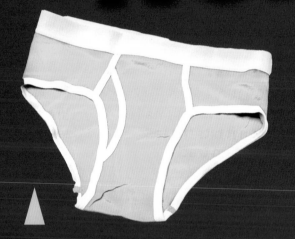

In **JAPAN,** drivers can be fined for the act of 'muddy driving' – splashing mud on a pedestrian by driving through a puddle!

In the city of **SAN FRANCISCO, USA,** you're not allowed to clean your car with used underwear (but it's totally fine to use new undies)!

In **SWITZERLAND,** you are not allowed to wash your car on a Sunday.

In **GERMANY FRANCE** and **SPAIN,** you can fined for driving wh wearing flip-flops.

In **CYPRUS,** it's illegal to eat or drink anything at all while you're driving – even taking a sip of water could land you with a fine!

In the **PHILIPPINES,** cars with number plates ending in a 1 or 2 aren't allowed on the roads on Mondays, number plates ending 3 or 4 on Tuesday and so on up to Friday!

In the **UK,** shouting, making rude gestures to other drivers or honking unnecessarily could get you fined £1,000.

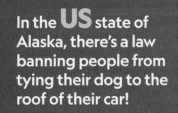

In the **US** state of Alaska, there's a law banning people from tying their dog to the roof of their car!

Totally WEIRD!

In the state of Georgia in the USA, it's illegal to spit from a car or bus. It's fine if you're in a truck though!

107

The Graveyard of
THE ATLANTIC

There's an area of the ocean off the coast of North Carolina, USA, which has proved so dangerous to ships that it's earned the nickname the 'Graveyard of the Atlantic'. More than 2,000 vessels have met their doom there.

Early explorers ventured to the region because the mouth of the Cape Fear River opens out to the sea there. After the first recorded wreck – nearly 500 years ago, in 1526 – sailors soon realised how risky it was to travel these waters.

Legend says that in the eighteenth century the famous pirate Blackbeard learnt to navigate the tricky coastline here so he could escape capture – he knew others would be reluctant to follow him into such dangerous waters.

Almost every type of boat has ended its days in this ship graveyard – Spanish treasure ships, steamers, tankers, freighters, barges, clippers and even nippy little 'blockade runners' used to sneak goods in and out during the American Civil War. That's one reason why it's so popular with scuba divers, who love to explore the huge variety of wrecks.

It's also become an important place for marine archaeologists, who have recently been studying two particular wrecks. The *USS Tarpon* was a submarine used in World War II, which sank in 1956 while being towed off for scrap. The *Proteus* was a luxurious passenger liner that travelled between New York and New Orleans. One dark night in 1918, it collided with a tanker and sank to the ocean floor. Today these wrecks are home to all sorts of interesting sea creatures and marine plants, establishing life in a once-human space.

Did you KNOW?

Despite his skill as a sailor and his knowledge of the area, Blackbeard's ship *Queen Anne's Revenge* is one of the wrecks in the Graveyard of the Atlantic! Blackbeard himself survived the disaster but died a bloody death in battle a few months later.

Cool CANALS

ANCIENT WATERWAYS

The **OLDEST** canal in the UK is nearly 2,000 years old! The **FOSSDYKE NAVIGATION** was built by the Romans in around CE 120 and is still used today. But that's young compared to the Beijing–Hangzhou Grand Canal in China, which was built in 468 BCE – the oldest canal in the world.

◀ DREDGING DISCOVERIES

People throw some weird things into canals. Items **DREDGED UP** from Britain's canals include cars, golf buggies, shopping trollies, frying pans, unexploded bombs and grenades from the Second World War, and even a 5-metre-long python!

TERRAPIN TERROR!

Red-eared **TERRAPINS** became popular pets in the 1980s thanks to the Teenage Mutant Ninja Hero Turtles. When they got too big (they grow to about the size of a dinner plate!) lots of people released them into the wild. They've been breeding happily in the UK's canals ever since!

ANIMAL POWER

HORSES were originally used to pull cargo boats along. **TOWPATHS** were built alongside the canals for the animals to walk along, with a rope linking them to the boat. Even when boats began to be equipped with steam engines, people stuck to animal power because horses could still go faster!

TAKE YOUR TIME

The **LONGEST SETS OF LOCKS** on a canal in the UK is known as the **TARDEBIGGE FLIGHT.** With 30 locks along 3.6 kilometres of canal, it takes about 4.5 hours to get through them all!

HIGH-RISE TRAVEL

Along the Llangollen Canal, boats must make a precarious crossing over the 18-arch **PONTCYSYLLTE AQUEDUCT.** It was built in 1805 by the famous engineer Thomas Telford.

Totally WEIRD!

More than 15,000 people live permanently on narrowboats in the UK. It's a great life being able to move your home when you fancy a change of scenery (although it does make it difficult for the post person to find you!).

Out of this world

Of all the **PLANETS** in the **SOLAR SYSTEM**, only **TWO** have permanent **ICE CAPS** – **EARTH** and **MARS**.

CHAPTER 7

Launch yourself over to page 120 to discover more earthly features of the Solar System.

Third rock
FROM THE SUN

Let's start with some fast facts about the planet we call home.

Earth is the **THIRD** planet from the Sun and the **FIFTH** largest planet in the Solar System.

It's approximately **147 MILLION KILOMETRES** from the Sun, so light takes about 8 minutes and 19 seconds to reach us.

Earth **ISN'T A PERFECT SPHERE.** It's more like a squashed ball, bulging out at the Equator thanks to its spin and the force of gravity.

The Moon is not Earth's only companion. The asteroid **3753 CRUITHNE** takes the same time to orbit the Sun as Earth does, but its orbit is different so it looks as though Cruithne and Earth follow each other.

The **TEMPERATURE** at Earth's **CORE** is the same as the temperature on the **SURFACE OF THE SUN.**

Our planet is **15,000 TIMES OLDER THAN WE ARE!** Earth formed around 4.5 billion years ago and our species, *Homo sapiens,* has been here for around 300,000 years.

Earth is the only planet whose **NAME** does not come from Greek or Roman mythology. It simply means **'THE GROUND'** in Old English and Germanic languages.

The strength of **GRAVITY** isn't the same everywhere on Earth. It's weaker at the top of mountains, for example – and at the Equator.

NASA uses the Atacama Desert in Chile to practise techniques for searching for **LIFE ON MARS,** because it is so dry there.

Totally WEIRD!

Scientists think that over 5,000 kilograms of cosmic dust from space drifts down to Earth every year.

THE PILLARS OF CREATION

In 1995, five years after it was launched, the HUBBLE SPACE TELESCOPE (HST) sent an incredible picture back to Earth. It showed what looked like strange rock formations, but which are actually columns of dust and gas in the Eagle Nebula, a massive star-forming region of space 6,500 light-years from Earth.

The picture became world-famous, and the columns were named the 'Pillars of Creation', because deep in their dusty interior, new stars are being formed. In 2014, Hubble returned to take another picture of the pillars (shown above).

The colours in the picture represent different gases. Blue areas are oxygen, red are sulphur and green are nitrogen and hydrogen.

In 2022, the newly launched—and more powerful—JAMES WEBB SPACE TELESCOPE turned its eye towards the Pillars of Creation. The images it returned are much sharper than Hubble's and give us a better look inside the pillars. You can even see stars that are about to break free from their dusty prison.

The blue background in the Webb image shows area of hydrogen and it's filled with many more stars than the Hubble image was able to capture. The wavy lines shooting out from the edge of the pillars are supersonic jets fired out from stars that are still forming in the dust.

The new pictures will help scientists understand much more about how stars form from gas and dust over millions of years, and how they eventually burst out of their birthplaces such as these extraordinary pillars.

Did you KNOW

The Pillars of Creation are huge: 4–5 light-years long. But they're still only a small part of the Eagle Nebula, which covers an area 70 by 55 light-years

Houston, we have A PROBLEM...

On 20 July 1969, *Apollo 11* astronauts Neil Armstrong, Buzz Aldrin and Michael Collins became the first humans to visit the Moon. But not everything on that first visit went as planned!

ONE SMALL STEP?

Armstrong famously said he made 'one small step for man, one giant leap for mankind,' but his own step was bigger than expected! The lander was set down so gently that the struts didn't crush as much as planners thought. Armstrong had to jump down from the bottom rung to make that first step!

Totally WEIRD!

Moon dust smells! Armstrong and Aldrin didn't notice it when they were loping about on the lunar surface, but they were surprised by the strong odour when they got back in the module. They said it smelt like gunpowder or wet ash.

BLOWN AWAY

The *Apollo 11* astronauts planted a US flag on the Moon, but it didn't last long. As the lunar module took off again, Aldrin noticed that the blast sent the flag flying away. Later lunar astronauts learned a lesson and put their flags further away from the module!

A SIMPLE SOLUTION

Back on the lunar module, the astronauts realised to their horror that a switch controlling a circuit breaker had broken off the instrument panel. They couldn't lift off! Mission Control worked overnight, but still hadn't come up with anything when Aldrin solved the problem himself—by sticking a felt-tip pen where the switch had been!

GENERAL DECLARATION

(Outward/Inward)

AGRICULTURE, CUSTOMS, IMMIGRATION, AND PUBLIC HEALTH

Owner or Operator _____ NATIONAL AERONAUTICS AND SPACE ADMINISTRATION

Marks of Nationality and Registration _____ U.S.A. _____ Flight No. _____ APOLLO 11 _____ Date _____ JULY 24, 1969

Departure from _____ MOON _____ Arrival at _____ HONOLULU, HAWAII, U.S.A.
(Place and Country) _____ (Place and Country)

FLIGHT ROUTING

("Place" Column always to list origin, every en-route stop and destination)

PLACE	TOTAL NUMBER OF CREW	NUMBER OF PASSENGERS ON THIS STAGE	CARGO
CAPE KENNEDY	COMMANDER NEIL A. ARMSTRONG		
MOON		Departure Place:	
JULY 24, 1969 HONOLULU	COLONEL EDWIN E. ALDRIN, JR.	Embarking NIL Through on same flight NIL	MOON ROCK AND MOON DUST SAMPLES Cargo Manifests Attached
		Arrival Place:	
	LT. COLONEL MICHAEL COLLINS	Disembarking NIL Through on same flight NIL	

Declaration of Health

Persons on board known to be suffering from illness other than airsickness or the effects of accidents, as well as those cases of illness disembarked during the flight:

NONE

For official use only

HONOLULU AIRPORT
Honolulu, Hawaii
ENTERED

Customs Inspector

Any other condition on board which may lead to the spread of disease:

TO BE DETERMINED

Details of each disinsecting or sanitary treatment (place, date, time, method) during the flight. If no disinsecting has been carried out during the flight give details of most recent disinsecting:

Signed, if required _____ Crew Member Concerned

I declare that all statements and particulars contained in this General Declaration, and in any supplementary forms required to be presented with this General Declaration are complete, exact and true to the best of my knowledge and that all through passengers will continue/have continued on the flight.

WHERE ARE YOU FROM?

When they arrived back to Earth, the astronauts were taken to Hawaii. Just like any other traveller, they were asked to fill in a customs form saying where they were travelling from and to. What, they wondered, should they put in the 'Departure from' section? 'Moon,' of course!

Just like HOME

Our planet may be one of a kind in our Solar System when it comes to supporting life, but other planets and their moons have some familiar features.

TITAN'S LAKES

There are a lot of **LAKES** on Saturn's moon **TITAN**, but there's no water in them. Instead, they're filled with **METHANE** and **ETHANE.** On Earth these are gases, but on chilly Titan they are in the form of liquid.

MARS'S CANYON

The canyon system on Mars, **VALLES MARINERIS,** extends for 4,000 kilometres. That's **FIVE TIMES** the length of the **GRAND CANYON** here on Earth.

IO'S VOLCANOES

There's more **VOLCANIC ACTIVITY** on Jupiter's moon Io than anywhere else in the solar system. The volcanoes there shoot **SUPEHEATED GASES** more than 300 kilometres out into space.

THE MOON'S PLAINS

The plains on the Moon are called **MARIA**, which means 'sea', but they're actually made of smooth rock. They're caused by ancient **ASTEROID IMPACTS.**

ENCELADUS'S OCEAN

The surface of Saturn's moon Enceladus covers a **SECRET SEA** – an entire ocean of salty liquid. Vents in the crust allow **JETS** of water vapour, gases and ice particles to shoot hundreds of kilometres into space.

THE DAY THE UNIVERSE CHANGED

For hundreds of years, as far as anyone knew, our galaxy, the Milky Way, was the only one. But on 30 December 1924, astronomer Edwin Hubble changed our understanding of our place in the universe forever. He announced his discovery that the spiral nebula Andromeda was actually a galaxy, and that far from being unique, the Milky Way was one of many galaxies spread out across the universe.

Hubble had been studying what he believed were spiral nebulae using a powerful new telescope at Mount Wilson, California, USA. He—like everyone else—thought that these blurry blobs of light in the night sky were clouds of gas in our own galaxy.

But while studying the Andromeda nebula, he spotted something strange. Within it were some special stars called Cepheid variables, which vary in brightness. Prior to this, an astronomer called Henrietta Leavitt discovered that the time it took for these stars to change from bright to dim and back again was related to their brightness; this relationship could be used to measure how far away they were.

Hubble used Leavitt's discovery to work out the distance to Andromeda, and he was astonished by what he found. It was around 860,000 light-years away. That was much further than the most distant stars in the Milky Way. Andromeda wasn't a cloud of gas in our own galaxy. It was a whole separate star system—a galaxy in its own right.

Hubble went on to make many more amazing galaxy discoveries. He also identified the four different types of galaxies that astronomers still use to classify them today: spiral, barred spiral, elliptical and irregular. Hubble's amazing achievements were honoured when NASA named its first space telescope after him.

Totally WEIRD!

In the past 100 years, we've gone from believing we're the only galaxy in the universe to realising that there may be as many as 200 *billion* galaxies out there!

COLOURS of the COSMOS

Mars is nicknamed the **RED PLANET** thanks to iron minerals in its soil and rock. As these oxidise (rust), the rusty dust gets into the atmosphere and makes the sky look reddish.

BROWN DWARFS are made of the same stuff as stars, but they don't have enough mass to trigger the process of nuclear fusion, which is what makes stars bright.

The **RED SPIDER NEBULA** is home to one of the hottest known stars in the universe. Winds from the star shoot out waves that are 100 billion kilometres high!

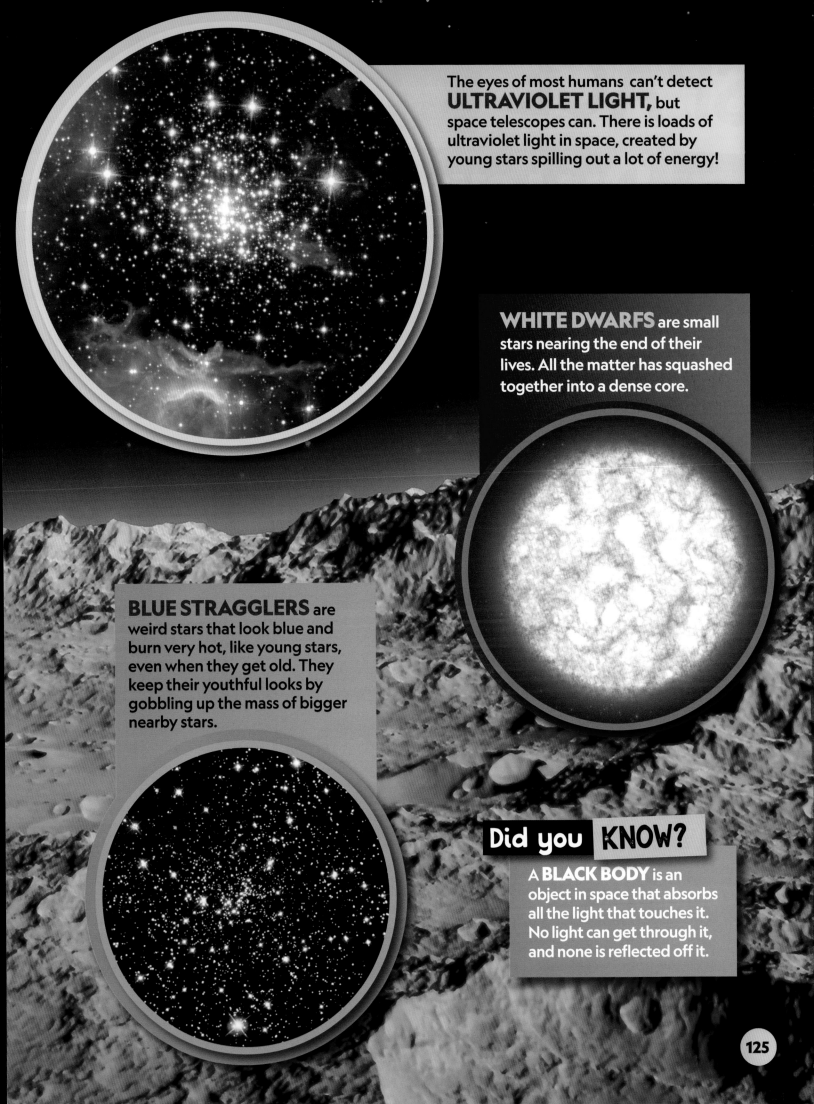

The eyes of most humans can't detect **ULTRAVIOLET LIGHT,** but space telescopes can. There is loads of ultraviolet light in space, created by young stars spilling out a lot of energy!

WHITE DWARFS are small stars nearing the end of their lives. All the matter has squashed together into a dense core.

BLUE STRAGGLERS are weird stars that look blue and burn very hot, like young stars, even when they get old. They keep their youthful looks by gobbling up the mass of bigger nearby stars.

Did you KNOW?

A **BLACK BODY** is an object in space that absorbs all the light that touches it. No light can get through it, and none is reflected off it.

SPACE
Dwarfs

So far, we know of only five dwarf planets in our Solar System. Let's meet the members of this exclusive gang.

THE LEADER

For 76 years after its discovery, **PLUTO** was proud to be known as the ninth planet. But in 2006, it was stripped of its title and reclassified as a dwarf planet. The biggest of the group, Pluto is only 2,377 kilometres across – smaller than Earth's Moon. It has five moons of its own!

Totally WEIRD!

A dwarf-planet like space body is the farthest-away object in our solar system. It's officially named 2018 AG37, but is mainly known by its nickname, Farfarout! It's so faraway that scientist think it takes a thousand years to orbit the Sun .

THE TROUBLEMAKER

Pluto can blame **ERIS** for its demotion into the dwarf planet category! When Eris was first discovered scientists thought it was bigger than Pluto (it's actually very slightly smaller). That got everyone wondering how to define these smaller worlds. Eris has a weak atmosphere of methane and nitrogen gases which are thought to fall as snow when Eris moves away from the Sun.

THE JOKER

HAUMEA spins on its axis faster than almost any other object in our Solar System – once every four hours. This super spin may have been set off by a collision with a larger object in the distant past. Scientists think that Haumea's odd egg shape might also be caused by the spinning speed!

THE OUTSIDER

Like Pluto, **CERES** joined the dwarf planets from another gang – to begin with, everyone thought it was an asteroid. In fact, it was the first 'asteroid' to be discovered, in 1801! It's the only dwarf planet to live in the Asteroid Belt rather than the Kuiper Belt.

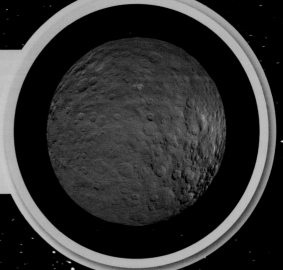

THE NEWCOMER

MAKEMAKE is the newest member of the group, found in 2005. It's named after the creator god in the Rapanui mythology of the people of Easter Island. The dwarf planet was discovered around Easter time, and before it was properly identified the research team referred to it by the name Easterbunny!

To the MOON and BACK

On 11 December 2022, NASA's *Orion* spacecraft came splashing down in the Pacific Ocean. The date marked the 50th anniversary of *Apollo 17* landing on the Moon—the last time humans touched down on the lunar surface. *Orion*'s successful return was the latest milestone in NASA's new programme, Artemis, which will eventually take humans back to the Moon—and beyond.

Before putting a human crew in *Orion*, NASA wanted to check that everything was working properly in deep space conditions. So, they sent the craft on a test mission, Artemis I.

Sitting in the boss's chair on *Orion* was Commander Moonikin Campos. Despite his title, the commander is not a real astronaut, but a manikin with special sensors to monitor the effects of space travel on the human body. He was dressed in the *Orion* Crew Survival System spacesuit, to make sure it worked. The commander's loyal companion on the journey was a soft-toy Snoopy. The cuddly dog was used as a zero-gravity indicator, showing when the spacecraft had reached weightlessness.

On 16 November 2022, Commander Campos, Snoopy and crew were launched into space on *Orion*. Their journey lasted 25 days and took them within 130 kilometres of the Moon's surface, before travelling deeper into space. At the farthest point, they were 435,000 kilometres from Earth. That's more than 1,000 times further than the International Space Station.

With a safe return to Earth, NASA will be able to use the information from the mission to make any adjustments necessary for the next stage—Artemis II. This 10-day crewed mission on *Orion* is planned for 2024.

Sporting
superstars

TENNIS star SERENA WILLIAMS has a STRANGE SUPERSTITION: if she is on a WINNING RUN, she DOESN'T CHANGE HER SOCKS!

Speed over to page 140 for more super sport superstitions.

Paris Olympics
then and now

The 2024 Olympics are being held in Paris, exactly 100 years since the city last hosted the Games.

1924

3,089 ATHLETES took part in the 1924 Paris Olympics— 2,954 men and 135 women.

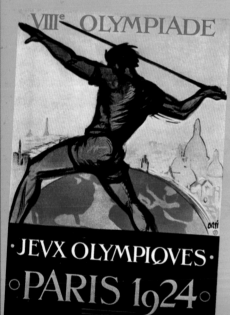

VIIIᵉ OLYMPIADE

· JEVX OLYMPIQVES ·
·PARIS 1924·

ART was an event at the 1924 Olympics! The founder of the modern Olympics, Pierre de Coubertin, believed the Games should combine **MUSCLES AND MIND.**

There were 17 sports on the programme, which was **FIVE LESS** than the previous Olympics in 1920. Archery, field hockey and tug-of-war were dropped. Figure skating and ice hockey were moved to the Winter Olympics.

Harold Abrahams winning the 100 metres.

Did you KNOW?

American swimmer JOHNNY WEISSMULLER won three gold medals, but he's more famous for his later career – playing Tarzan in no less than 12 films!

Approximately **10,500 ATHLETES** will take part in the 2024 Olympics and 4,400 in the Paralympics, with roughly equal numbers of men and women.

In 2024, between the Olympics and the Paralympics, Paris is hosting the **'CULTURAL OLYMPIAD'**, which celebrates the links between **ART** and **SPORT.**

PARiS 2024

For the first time in an Olympics, there will be running events open to amateurs, including the Mass Participation Marathon.

The age of athletes at the Olympics is decided by the international organisations for each sport. Competitors in 2024 could be as young as 12, like skateboarding silver medalist Kokona Hiraki, or in their sixties, like equestrian Mary Hanna, both of whom took part in the Tokyo 2020 Olympics.

One new sport was added to the Olympics for 2024 – **BREAKING** (breakdancing) – making a total of 32.

Fun on four WHEELS

SWAMP BUGGY RACING

SWAMP BUGGIES are often built from bits of old aeroplanes and tractors. The big tyres help the buggies race through the muddy water of swamps and marshes. The driver sits on a high platform to keep them as far away from the mud as possible!

Totally WEIRD!

The **PIG-N-FORD** race takes place every year at the Tillamook County Fair in Oregon, USA. Drivers have to crank up an early 1900s Model T Ford, grab a pig and do a lap of the course. They then pick up another pig and do another lap. The winner is the driver who completes three laps without a pig escaping!

LAWNMOWER RACING

LAWNMOWER RACING was invented in England by a group of people who wanted to find a cheap form of motor racing. The ride-on mowers are modified to make them safer – including removing the cutting blades!

FOLK RACING

This **SWEDISH FORM OF RALLY DRIVING** involves a lot of cheap, battered old cars that get even more dented as they race each other. The cars must have roll cages to protect the drivers because flip-overs happen a lot in folk racing!

STADIUM SUPER TRUCK RACING

In **STADIUM SUPER TRUCK RACING,** bouncy four-wheel drives race around a track overtaking each other any way they can. Sometimes they even jump right over each other!

ROCK CRAWLING

The aim of the game with **ROCK CRAWLING** is to get round the course as quickly as possible without damaging the vehicle. To make them rock-proof, they're usually modified jeeps or similar strong vehicles, with big tyres and brilliant suspension!

Sport of WIZARDS

When J.K. Rowling dreamed up the sport Quidditch for the *Harry Potter* books, she probably never imagined that it would become a real sport one day. After all, a game played by wizards zooming around in the air on broomsticks and involving a tiny ball that flies around on its own is a tough one for muggles (non-wizards) to take on! But in 2005, students at a college in the USA came up with a version of Quidditch—now known as Quadball—that can be played on the ground.

Each team has seven players—with a maximum of four of the same gender. The players all must keep a broomstick between their legs throughout the match. The quaffle (a volleyball) is used to score goals, worth 10 points, as players try to get it through three hoops at the ends of the pitch. There are also three bludgers (dodgeballs), which can be chucked at opposing players. If a player is hit with a bludger, they're said to have been knocked off their broom. They have to run back to their own goal, before remounting and re-joining the match.

And the golden snitch? That's a tennis ball in a sock, tucked into the waistband of a player's shorts! This player, the Snitch Runner, works alone. Dressed in yellow, they race around on and off the pitch. They're allowed to dodge and weave, hide, climb trees, even escape by bicycle—anything to stop the teams' Seekers from stealing the snitch! Getting hold of the snitch scores that team 30 points and marks the end of the game.

137

Sporting FIRSTS

FIRST TOUR DE FRANCE

The Tour de France launched in Paris on 1 July 1903 and ended in the same city two and half weeks later. Frenchman Maurice Garin took the title after cycling the 2,428-kilometre race in 94 hours, 33 minutes, and 14 seconds.

FIRST WIMBLEDON

The first ever Wimbledon Tennis Championships were held in July 1877. Only men competed and Brit Spencer Gore won the trophy. The first women's championship was held in 1884. It was won by Maud Watson, who beat her own sister, Lilian, in the final!

FIRST GRAND PRIX

In June 1906, 32 cars lined up in Le Mans, France to mark the start of the first motor racing Grand Prix. Only 11 of them finished! Hungarian driver Ferenc Szisz took the title with an average speed of 101 kilometres per hour. Today's Formula One drivers average 366 kilometres per hour at Le Mans!

The yellow jersey traditionally worn by the leader of the Tour de France was introduced in 1919. The colour was a nod to the newspaper that sponsored the race, which was printed on yellow paper. The first yellow jersey was also made of wool – which must have been very sweaty to cycle in!

FIRST WORLD CUP

The first FIFA World Cup whistle blew on 13 July 1930, in Uruguay. Ten days later, the hosts beat Argentina 4–2 in the first ever World Cup Final. There was no official ball in those days and the teams argued over whose ball to use! Argentina won the toss and the game kicked off with their ball.

FIRST SUPER BOWL

The first American football Super Bowl was played on 15 January 1967, with the Green Bay Packers beating the Kansas City Chiefs 35–10. It was known as the AFL-NFL World Championship Game at the time – the much snappier 'Super Bowl' wasn't officially adopted until the third annual game.

STRANGE SPORTING SUPERSTITIONS

Champion golfer **TIGER WOODS** always wears a red shirt when he plays on Sundays.

Superstar tennis champion **RAFAEL NADAL** has two water bottles, which he arranges in a particular way. He takes alternate sips from each bottle between games.

Some **BASEBALL PLAYERS** believe that spitting in their hand before they pick up the bat will bring them luck.

Footballer **CRISTIANO RONALDO** always steps onto the pitch with his right leg first.

 US judo star **KAYLA HARRISON** always wore a pair of 'lucky' socks that her grandma gave her.

Totally WEIRD!

In ICE HOCKEY, it's thought to be bad luck if hockey sticks are left lying crossed over.

Czech snowboarder **EVA ADAMCZYKOVÁ** draws a fake moustache on her upper lip to bring her luck in important competitions.

After basketball superstar **MICHAEL JORDAN'S** college team won a 1982 championship, Jordan decided that his blue shorts were lucky. He wore them under his other shorts for the rest of his career!

Dive in the DEEP END

Charlotte Sanddal didn't start swimming until she was 72. At 100 years old, she was still breaking records, including five world records in Masters swimming competitions!

WHERE DID EVERYONE GO?!

Solo synchronised swimming was introduced as an Olympic event in 1984. Right from the start people thought it was strange – who were the solo swimmers synchronised with?! Olympic organisers dropped it after 1992.

SWEATY SWIMMERS

Just like other athletes, swimmers sweat. Although the water keeps them a bit cooler than athletes on dry land, they're still sweating into the pool. Things get especially sticky under that swimming cap.

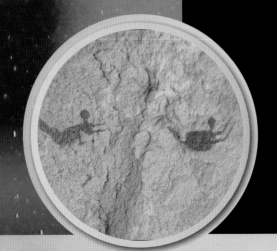

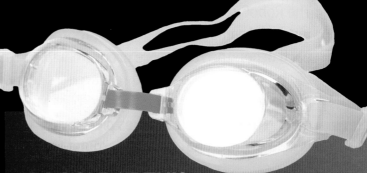

GOGGLE AT THIS

Swimming goggles were invented in Persia (modern-day Iran) in the fourteenth century. Pearl divers carved them out of tortoise shell which was both waterproof and see-through, to help them see more clearly while searching for their underwater treasure.

PROOF OF AN ANCIENT PASTIME

Ancient cave art in Egypt suggests that people have enjoyed swimming for thousands of years. The caves contain a series of underground pools, which the ancient Egyptians may have swum in for leisure as well using for religious rituals.

TAKE A DEEP BREATH

Free divers swim underwater without any special equipment such as oxygen tanks. And they can hold their breath for amazing lengths of time. Croatian free diver Budimir Šobat held his breath underwater for charity in 2021 – and achieved a world record of 24 minutes 37.36 seconds!

The FUTURE of FOOTBALL?

The RoboCup is a robotics competition that involves teams of robots playing football against each other. The robots are programmed by teams of students, engineers and researchers to move around the field, kick the ball and try to score goals. The competition takes place every year and is held in different countries around the world.

The first RoboCup took place in Japan in 1997 and has been held nearly every year since then. More than 40 countries now send teams to battle it out on the RoboCup pitch! There are different leagues for different types of robots, including small, medium and humanoid.

But the RoboCup isn't just about creating an unbeatable robotic team or even simply enjoying a game of footie. It's also about using robotics and artificial intelligence (AI) to solve real-world problems. By developing robots that can play football, teams can also help to improve how robots work in other areas, such as emergency rescue, manufacturing and healthcare. This is one sporting competition that's about more than just the game!

When it started, the competition organisers had an ambitious goal in mind. By 2050, they wanted a team of humanoid robots to be so good at football that they'd be able to beat the latest winners of the (human) World Cup. So far, robots are a way off from being able to take on world-class human teams like Argentina or France. But 2050 is a while away yet, so who knows what the future holds for footballing robots!

Did you KNOW?

As well as the football competition, there are other types of challenge, including 'rescue'. Teams of robots must navigate through pretend disasters, performing tasks such as searching for and rescuing victims, identifying hazards and mapping the environment.

Coolly creative

JAUME PLENSA is a 'VISUAL ARTIST' most famous for his SCULPTURES of huge human figures made of LETTERS and NUMBERS. He makes sculptures out of lots of different materials, including STAINLESS STEEL, MARBLE and GLASS.

Stroll over to page 150 to admire some more strange sculptures.

SING IT LOUD!

PREHISTORIC MELODIES

PREHISTORIC PEOPLE may have been singing even before spoken language developed. Musical sounds could have been used to express emotions and copy the sounds of nature.

HAPPY BIRTHDAY

Singing 'Happy Birthday' may make your celebration cake taste better. A study by Harvard University and the University of Minnesota concluded that taking part in this birthday ritual before indulging in cake can increase your enjoyment of the food.

Totally WEIRD!

International Strange Music Day is on 24 August. It was launched by musician Patrick Grant in 1997 as a way to get people to listen to his new album. Today, it encourages people to listen to music that they might not know or think they like!

ASTRONAUT

ASTRONAUT Chris Hadfield recorded some album songs while he was on the International Space Station. He called it Space Sessions: Songs from a Tin Can.

JUKEBOX

The reason that the music charts on radio usually consist of the TOP 40 songs may be because in the 1950s most JUKEBOXES could store 40 songs.

SPICE GIRLS

On average people can recognise a popular song from its introduction in about 5 seconds. But in one study, people started singing along to 'Wannabe' by the Spice Girls in an average 2.34 seconds. That might make it the CATCHIEST SONG EVER!

THE BEATLES

THE BEATLES were popular in the 1960s and are still one of the most famous bands ever. But not one of the Fab Four band members could read or write music!

MARIAH CAREY

Mariah Carey **INSURED HER VOICE** for a whopping $35 million just in case something happened and she couldn't make a living from singing any more.

Outdoor ART

GUARDIAN ANGEL ▶

THE ANGEL OF THE NORTH, in northern England, is the largest angel sculpture in the world. Its outstretched wings measure more than most passenger planes, and it contains enough steel to make 16 double decker buses!

◀ GIVE ME A HAND

In the Atacama Desert in Chile a huge hand reaches up, as if a giant is trying to surface from the sand! The **HAND OF THE DESERT** is made of concrete and iron and stands twice as high as an average house.

▼ CAR GRAVEYARD

CADILLAC RANCH is made up of ten old American cars called Cadillacs, which were partly buried in a field in 1974. People are allowed to paint and write on the cars so they're often brightly coloured!

STOP OR GO? ▶

London's **TRAFFIC LIGHT TREE** would be very confusing if it was really directing traffic. Although the 75 sets of lights change between red, amber, and green in the usual pattern, it's actually a piece of amazing art.

BEWARE OF MONSTERS

The **PARK OF THE MONSTERS** in Italy is famous for its strange sculptures. The figures of animals, monsters and other fantastical creatures were carved into the natural rock formations in the sixteenth century.

Did you KNOW?

Huge SHUTTLECOCKS have taken a nosedive into the grounds of an art museum in Kansas, USA. Not everyone liked them at first, but now they're a popular visitor attraction!

Bryan Berg
CARD ARCHITECT!

Bryan Berg is a card stacking artist, which means that he builds amazing structures using just playing cards! Starting with a few cards, card stackers like Bryan slowly and carefully place other cards on top of them to create mini versions of famous buildings and even ones that they've designed themselves.

Bryan started playing around with playing cards when he was at school. Now he's a world record holder for card stacking. One of these records – the largest playing-card structure in the world – was a replica of three buildings in Macau, China, which took him 44 days to construct. Another of his world records is for the largest house of freestanding playing cards. For that, he recreated Cinderella's Castle from Disney World, using around 156,000 cards! He's created many other incredible card buildings for both work and fun, including the Eiffel Tower and the Great Wall of China.

One reason that Bryan is such a genius at card stacking is that he studied architecture, so he understands how to design and build structures that won't collapse. Some of his card buildings are strong enough to support bricks and won't blow down even in quite strong winds.

He proved how sturdy his card structures are with another record – the tallest house of cards built in 12 hours. Bryan stacked 48 storeys of cards on top of a washing machine, while it was running! Amazingly, the tower stayed standing. This particular record was broken in 2022 by another cool card stacker, Tian Rui, who built a 50-storey house. He started from the floor though!

Totally WEIRD!

Bryan built a model hotel out of key cards that are used to open hotel-room doors! It had human-size beds and furniture like bedside tables and lamps.

Potty for Pottery

ANCIENT CRAFT

The wheel that potters use to shape pots and other pieces was invented in **ANCIENT MESOPOTAMIA** more than 6,000 years ago. Every ancient civilisation figured out how to use clay to make pots and other items.

STRANGE CLAY

The **STRANGE CLAY EXHIBITION** put a new twist on the ancient art of ceramics. Instead of bowls and pots, artists displayed fun decorative pieces and ones with messages about our modern world.

NOBODY DID IT!

MR NOBODY was a popular ceramic figure in the seventeenth century. His legs joined directly to his head—that's why he was **MR NO-BODY!** People blamed the figure when they had done something wrong: *WHO DID THAT? NOBODY!*

SAVE IT FOR LATER

The **ANCIENT EGYPTIANS** used pottery when making mummies. They believed that people would need their organs in the afterlife, so body parts like the stomach, liver and lungs were preserved in clay pots called **CANOPIC JARS.**

HILL OF ANCIENT JUGS

In ancient Rome, big pottery jars called **AMPHORAE** were used to store olive oil. When they were empty, people chucked them in a pile in the south of the city. The broken pieces grew into a huge hill, **50 METRES HIGH,** made of an estimated **53 MILLION AMPHORAE!**

CHIGGER CHIPS

A **CHIGGER BITE** is a tiny chip in a pot that removes the glaze but doesn't go as deep as the clay. It's named after the bite of the chigger mite. These teeny bugs are so small that they can't be seen with the naked eye, but their bites are incredibly itchy.

Did you KNOW?

The biggest clay pot ever was baked in Botswana. Art teacher Mmala Oefile started the Big Pot Africa project in 2018, but thanks to COVID lockdowns it wasn't until 2020 that the giant pot – as tall as two men – was finally finished!

Don't judge a BOOK by its cover

More than **160 MILLION BOOKS** have been published since the printing press was invented in the fifteenth century.

Dorothy Straight wrote a book called *How the World Began* when she was just four years old! It was published two years later, in 1964.

Teeny Ted from Turnip Town wins the prize for being the world's smallest book. Measuring just 70 by 100 micrometres (one thousandth of a millimetre), you need a special microscope to read it!

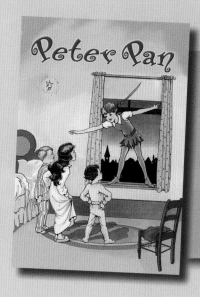

Author J. M. Barrie gave the copyright in his popular story **Peter Pan** to Great Ormond Street Children's Hospital in London. The money made from sales of the book and performances of the play still help the hospital today.

The fastest-selling book ever is *Harry Potter and the Deathly Hallows,* which sold 8.3 million copies in the first 24 hours after it was released!

The first novel ever written on a typewriter was *The Adventures of Tom Sawyer* by Mark Twain, which was written in 1876. At least, that's what Twain himself claimed!

Bestselling novelist Dan Brown, who wrote *The Da Vinci Code,* hangs upside down from gym equipment to help him when he's struggling for ideas!

Totally WEIRD!

Fear of running out of things to read is called abibliophobia. And the good feeling you get from the smell of old books is bibliosmia!

What were books called before they were books? The first use of the word *boc*, to mean a collection of written words bound together, was in a book translated by English King Alfred in the eighth century.

Who are YOU?

Not all creative people like being in the spotlight!

MYSTERIOUS MUSICIANS

Electronic music duo **Daft Punk** didn't keep their names a secret, but they rarely revealed their faces. On stage, they always wore masks that looked like robot helmets. They even wore the masks when they were being interviewed for television or magazines! They said it helped them to be more creative.

SECRETIVE STREET ARTIST

The street artist known as **Banksy** creates thought-provoking artworks that often have a political or social message. Although he's one of the most famous street artists in the world, nobody knows who Banksy really is! It is thought that he often works at night or wears a disguise so people don't see or recognise him.

ALL ABOUT THE ART

Felipe Pantone is a modern artist who loves using bright colours and geometric patterns. He's become very famous, but not many people would recognise him. He says that when people search for him online, he wants them to only see his art, as this will tell his fans more about him than his face will!

JANE EYRE.

An Autobiography.

EDITED BY
CURRER BELL.

IN THREE VOLUMES.
VOL. I.

LONDON:
SMITH, ELDER, AND CO., CORNHILL.
1847.

PEN NAMES

Charlotte, **Emily** and **Anne Brontë** published their famous books using the names **Currer**, **Ellis** and **Acton Bell**. This was partly because they thought not as many people would buy them if they knew they were written by women. It was also because some details in their stories were based on real people and events, so they thought it was better to stay anonymous!

Totally WEIRD!

Fashion designer Martin Margiela has preferred to remain anonymous for most of his career. In a documentary film about his life you can hear his voice and see his hands but not once does he show his face!

Singing in the rain ♪

Hidden away in the student district in the city of Dresden, Germany, is a group of courtyards called the Kunsthofpassage (art courtyards). Each of the five courtyards is designed on a different theme: the elements, animals, light, mythical creatures and metamorphoses (which means changing from one form to another). The buildings here are decorated in bright colours and unusual ways!

The most famous building is the 'Singing House', in the Courtyard of the Elements. Some of the people who live in the apartments here designed an extraordinary feature that covers the outside of the building – a zigzagging system of gutters, pipes, spouts and funnels that makes music when it rains! One of the designers thought of it.

Rain is caught in the gutters by the roof of the building, then channelled through the metal pipes, which amplifies the noise. The different shapes of the pipes make different singing sounds. There are even little waterfalls, platforms and a trumpet!

Did you KNOW?

The design of the Singing House was inspired by Rube Goldberg machines. These contraptions use different objects connected in a particular way to create a chain reaction that performs a simple task.

Buildings in the other courtyards each have their own style.

▶ In the **Courtyard of Animals,** a giant giraffe looks up as monkeys leap over it.

Designs for the **Courtyard of Light** were opened up in a national competition and people voted for the winner. The weirdly shaped metal mirrors reflect the Sun in different ways. ▲

Colourful painting and mosaics cover the walls in the **Courtyard of Mythical Creatures.** ▶

Grub's up

What was the **BEST THING** before SLICED BREAD? WRAPPED BREAD! Before bread was sold wrapped up in paper it went stale very quickly, so packaging it up to keep it fresh was considered a genius idea at the time!

Pack a sandwich and head over to page 170 for more brilliant bread facts.

Brilliant BISCUITS

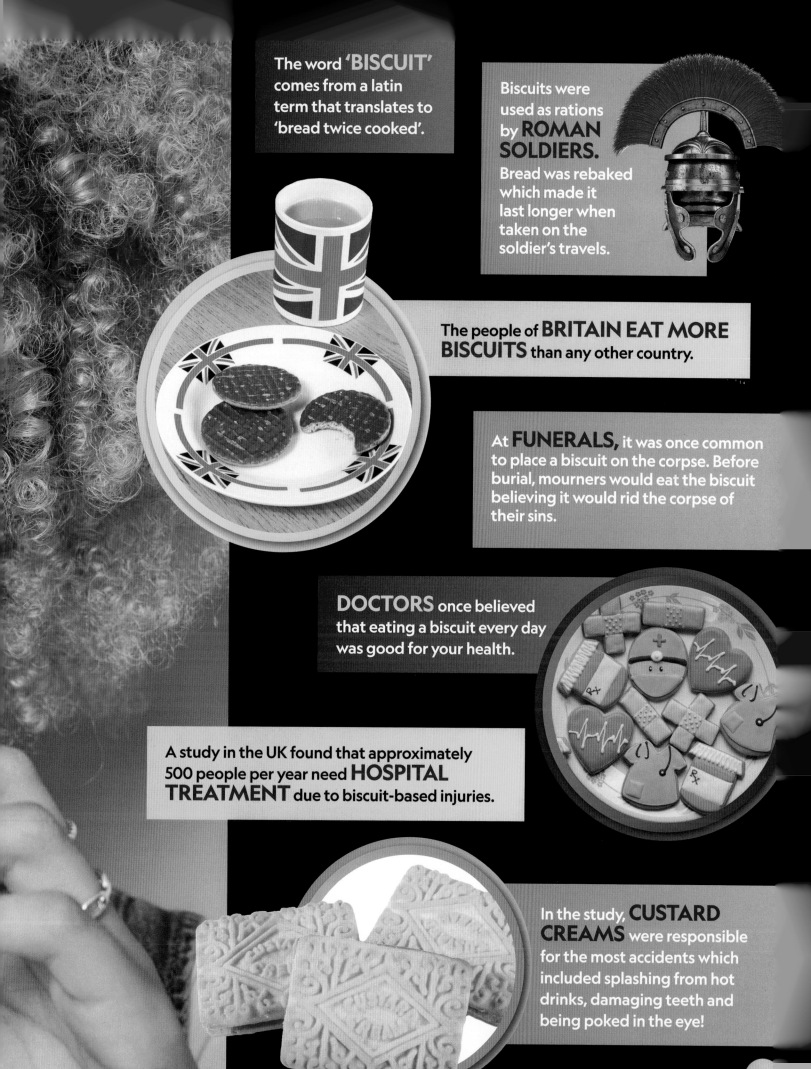

The word 'BISCUIT' comes from a latin term that translates to 'bread twice cooked'.

Biscuits were used as rations by ROMAN SOLDIERS. Bread was rebaked which made it last longer when taken on the soldier's travels.

The people of BRITAIN EAT MORE BISCUITS than any other country.

At FUNERALS, it was once common to place a biscuit on the corpse. Before burial, mourners would eat the biscuit believing it would rid the corpse of their sins.

DOCTORS once believed that eating a biscuit every day was good for your health.

A study in the UK found that approximately 500 people per year need HOSPITAL TREATMENT due to biscuit-based injuries.

In the study, CUSTARD CREAMS were responsible for the most accidents which included splashing from hot drinks, damaging teeth and being poked in the eye!

Unique
FOOD FESTIVALS

SQUASHED TOMATOES

LA TOMATINA takes place every year in the town of Buñol in Spain. The festival starts with a parade, where people dress up in costumes and play music. Then, at 11 am, a cannon is fired to signal the start of the main event – a huge tomato fight! An hour later, the cannon signals the end of the juicy battle.

HOPPING MAD

It's not only the French who love frogs' legs. In Florida, USA, the town of Fellsmere hosts the **FROG LEG FESTIVAL** every January. You can try a leg on a stick like a lollipop, served with coleslaw, or enjoy a whole heap of frogs' legs on their own. And if you don't fancy that, you can always try an alligator tail instead!

HUNGRY SPIRITS

The **HUNGRY GHOST FESTIVAL** is celebrated in parts of Asia on the fifteenth night of the seventh month. Although people celebrate with a delicious dinner themselves, most food is reserved for special guests – the ghosts of their ancestors. People believe the spirits have been wandering since the start of Hungry Ghost Month, two weeks earlier.

Totally WEIRD!

In Iceland, people celebrate a whole month of the Ugly Food Festival! Alongside typical Icelandic food such as fish and rye bread, people serve up boiled sheep's head, rotten shark and liver pudding.

VEGETABLE ART

During **LA NOCHE DE RÁBANOS** (the Night of the Radishes), people in Oaxaca, Mexico, gather to create sculptures out of – you guessed it – radishes! Competitors spend all day carving the purple vegetables into animals, people, buildings and even copies of famous paintings. In the evening, the entries are judged, and the winner is announced.

BLOOMING
chocolate

Have you ever opened a bar of chocolate and noticed that it's starting to turn white?

This white 'bloom' is completely harmless. It's caused by the cocoa butter, a type of liquid fat, travelling through the chocolate and forming crystals on the surface. However, that mouldy-looking white crust is enough to put off even the biggest chocolate lover – and chocolate-makers know it. They tried for years to figure out how to stop the white bloom appearing, but the problem really had them baffled! The trouble was that they didn't know exactly how the process took place, or how to stop it.

A group of scientists had a bright idea. Why not use X-rays to look inside the chocolate to see what was going on? This was easier to do if the chocolate wasn't solid, so first they mixed up the basic ingredients of chocolate into a powder. They added drops of sunflower oil to the powder and powered up the X-ray machine.

Thy could clearly see the oil moving – very quickly – through the chocolate. It worked its way through the *really* tiny spaces in the chocolate, called pores. As this happened, the chocolate itself lost some of its crystalline structure. The result of that is a brittle, chalky texture, instead of the yummy melt-in-your-mouth texture we all love in chocolate.

The scientists realised that reducing the number of pores in the chocolate while making it would slow the movement of the fat. It also helps to keep chocolate cool, to limit the amount of liquid fat in it.

Did you KNOW?

You can get rid of white bloom on chocolate simply by tempering it – that is, melting and cooling it again. Tempering chocolate by a quick blast in the microwave will restore its crystalline structure and remove the white markings.

BRING ON THE BREAD

The **LONGER YOU CHEW** a piece of bread, the **SWEETER IT TASTES.** That's because your saliva breaks down the starch in the bread and they become sugars.

Did you KNOW?

In medieval times, people used a flat, round piece of thick bread as a plate, called a **TRENCHER.** At the end of the meal, they'd gobble the plate up too!

Before erasers were invented, people used small, rolled-up pieces of bread or breadcrumbs to **RUB OUT PENCIL MARKS.**

Is it just bad luck that toast always seems to fall **JAM SIDE DOWN** when you drop it? Actually, it's all about the maths. From an average height, toast usually only has time to rotate one and a half times, so there's an 80% chance the jam side will hit the floor.

In ancient Rome, serving your guests bread made from **FINE FLOUR** showed that you were wealthy. They often cheated by mixing **ASHES** in with the flour to make it finer!

SANDWICHES are named after Sir John Montagu, the fourth Earl of Sandwich, who started a fashion for eating slices of meat between two pieces of bread or toast.

In some cultures, people throw bread at **WEDDINGS** to wish the wedding couple good luck.

The ancient Egyptians used **MOULDY BREAD** to treat burns that had become infected. This probably worked quite well because — as we now know — mould has an antibiotic effect.

Totally WEIRD!

The world's **LARGEST LOAF OF BREAD** was baked in Brazil in 2008. It weighed 1,571 kilograms - that's about the same as a hippo!

Do you believe these SUPERSTITIONS?

ONE IN THE EYE FOR THE DEVIL

If you spill salt, take a pinch of it, and throw it over your left shoulder with your right hand. This is said to blind the devil and stop him coming for you!

KEEP YOUR DISTANCE

Never hand your friend a hot pepper directly. Always put it on the table or on a plate and make sure they pick it up themselves. Otherwise, you'll fall out with that friend – or so the superstition says!

PEEL PREDICTION

Start at the top of an apple and peel it for as long as you can before the long piece of skin breaks. Throw the peeled skin on the table. The shape it forms is the first letter of the name of the person you will marry.

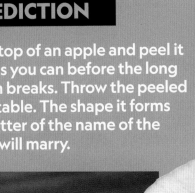

GRAPES AT MIDNIGHT

In Spain, there's a tradition of eating 12 grapes at the 12 chimes of midnight on New Year's Eve. If the grape is sweet, that month will be a good one. If the grape is sour, it'll be bad.

SORCERY AT SEA

Sailors once believed that witches used eggshells as boats and used their magic to cause havoc on the seas. To prevent this, people would smash the ends of their boiled eggs when they had finished eating them.

LO-O-ONG NOODLES

In some parts of China, noodles are said to symbolise long life. That's why people don't cut up their noodles but try to keep them whole as they suck them up!

Did you KNOW?

People once thought that rubbing an onion on a wart then throwing it over your shoulder would get rid of the wart and stop it from coming back!

FOOD CONFUSION

BREAKFAST BAKERY

CROISSANTS weren't invented in France and **DANISH PASTRIES** don't come from Denmark. Croissants were originally called Kipferi and were created in Vienna, Austria. It's thought that the Danish pastry was first created by a French baker who made a mistake in the making of dough but the result proved extra tasty!

FRUIT SALAD?

Scientifically speaking, **CUCUMBERS** are a fruit, not a vegetable, because they contain seeds and grow from the flower of a plant. Vegetables are usually the roots, stems and leaves of the plant.

NUT NONSENSE

PEANUTS aren't nuts. They're a type of plant called a legume, like peas, beans and lentils. The 'nut' in the hard shell is actually a seed.

RHUBARB PIE

Although it's often used in sweet dishes like pies and crumbles, **RHUBARB** is a vegetable because it's the stem of the plant. It's popular in savoury dishes too, such as curries and chutneys.

MODERN MILKS

Lots of people use almond, soy, or rice **MILKS** instead of milk from animals. But despite their name, these aren't really milk. After all, you can't milk a nut! They're made by soaking the nuts, soy, or rice in water, then blending them so they have the same look and texture as milk.

Did you KNOW?

Cauliflowers aren't always white. They come in purple, orange and green varieties as well!

Sweet
TALK

CANDY FLOSS has two key ingredients – sugar and air! Originally it was white, but later food colouring was added to brighten up the sweet treat.

KIT KATS are so popular in Japan that they have been made in hundreds of different flavours, including apple, green bean, strawberry cheesecake and soy sauce!

SNICKERS bars are named after the favourite horse of the Mars family, who started making the chocolate bar in 1930.

Did you KNOW?

The **WORLD'S OLDEST SWEET SHOP,** known as Ichiwa, opened in Kyoto, Japan. More than 1,000 years and 24 generations later, it's still being run by the same family.

Milk and dark chocolate contain cocoa solids, or 'nibs', which are what make chocolate, chocolate. **WHITE CHOCOLATE** contains cocoa butter but no solids, so technically it isn't chocolate.

JELLY BABIES were invented by mistake. The sweet maker was asked to make a mould for jelly bears, but it didn't come out quite right and the sweets looked more like babies!

Eat in or TAKE AWAY?

BATHROOM DINING

In the **MODERN TOILET RESTAURANT** in Taiwan, people sit on toilet seat chairs at tables made of sinks covered in glass tops. The rooms are tiled like a bathroom. There are showers on the walls and the lights are shaped like poo. Even some of the food is served in mini toilets!

CAFÉ CULTURE

Cream teas, including scones with jam and cream, are a traditional favourite for Brits and tourists alike. Visitors to National Trust properties in the UK eat more than **TWO MILLION SCONES** every year, as well as enjoying more than five million cups of tea and coffee in their cafés!

FAST FOOD FIT FOR A QUEEN

The **FIRST PIZZA DELIVERY** was made in 1889. Queen Margherita of Italy was tired of eating out every night while touring the country and asked for some traditional food to be delivered. A famous local pizza chef brought her a pizza with tomato, basil and mozzarella – the colours of the Italian flag. This simple pizza is still known as a Margherita.

CURRY FAVOURITE

The UK's favourite curry wasn't created in India. **CHICKEN TIKKA MASALA** is thought to have been invented in Scotland by the chef Ali Ahmed Aslam. He came up with the curry in the 1970s after one of his customers asked him if he could make the chicken tikka dish less dry. In response, he created a tomato-based sauce and cooked the tikka in it.

Did you KNOW?

The online food delivery company Just Eat reported that in 2021, it took over one billion orders around the world!

CHOPSTICKS that trick your taste buds

Salt is an essential ingredient in cooking. It adds flavour to all sorts of recipes. It's also important to help preserve food because bacteria can't survive in lots of salt. But there's also a problem with salt—too much of it is bad for us. So, for a long time, food companies have been trying to cut down on the amount of salt they put in their products.

A group of researchers in Japan tried to tackle the problem from a different angle. How could they help people who love the taste of salt in their food but need to cut down on the amount they eat? The ingenious solution that they came up with was 'smart' chopsticks, which add a salty flavour to food as it's eaten.

Salt is a mineral made up of ions of the elements sodium and chloride. Ions are particles that have a tiny electrical charge—and that's key to how the chopsticks work!

The chopsticks are linked to a type of watch or wristband which contains a tiny computer. As you pick up food with the chopsticks, the computer uses a small electrical current to pick up sodium ions in the food. They move through the chopsticks to your mouth, where the salty taste is increased. That means you can have less salt in the food but still get the same amount of flavour.

Maybe one day, all cutlery will be computer-controlled to improve the flavour of our food!

Totally WEIRD!

The same team that came up with the smart chopsticks also invented a TV screen that mimics the flavours of food being shown. The idea was for people to be able to lick the screen to get a taste of what was on the TV!

The human body

HAIR found at crime scenes can be the secret to SOLVING CRIMES. Analysing hair can show what was in a victim's BLOODSTREAM recently and what kind of ENVIRONMENT they lived in, as well as being used to identify SUSPECTS!

CHAPTER 11

Head over to page 192 for more hairy facts.

You can't!

YOU CAN'T SNEEZE WITH YOUR EYES OPEN

Despite the superstition, your eyeballs won't pop out if you **SNEEZE WITH YOUR EYES OPEN.** However, it's actually very hard to do, as your eyes close naturally when you sneeze. That may be your body's way of protecting your eyes from the irritating particles you're getting rid of through the sneeze!

YOU CAN'T READ AND LISTEN AT THE SAME TIME

Scientists think that it might be impossible to **LISTEN** to someone talk and perform a visual task, like reading a book or looking at your phone, at the same time. Hearing and vision use the same part of the brain, so doing the two things at once might simply be too much!

Totally WEIRD!

7 out of 10 people can roll their tongue.

1 in 10 people can touch their nose with the tip of their tongue.

3–4 in 10 people can raise one eyebrow.

1–2 people in 10 can wiggle their ears.

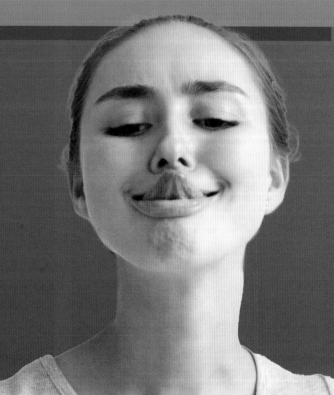

YOU CAN'T TICKLE YOURSELF

When someone TICKLES you, you get the giggles because you're not controlling the movement—it takes you by surprise! When you move any part of your own body, your brain knows in advance what feelings that movement will cause, so it doesn't really react.

YOU CAN'T HUM WHILE HOLDING YOUR NOSE

When you HUM, your mouth is closed. But while humming you're exhaling (letting out) air. If you hold your nose at the same time, there's nowhere for the air to go. After a couple of seconds you'll have to open your mouth SO YOU CAN BREATHE.

REMEMBER this!

A **PETABYTE** is one thousand million million bytes. Your amazing memory could **STORE UP TO 2.5 PETABYTES OF INFORMATION –** that's about the same as three million hours of TV programmes!

SHORT-TERM MEMORIES stick with you for an average of 30 seconds—then they're gone forever. But you can turn them into long-term memories by **ADDING INFORMATION** to them before they disappear.

LONG-TERM MEMORIES will last, but you must revisit them occasionally to keep them in your mind. Your brain forms long-term memories while you're asleep!

Your **PROCEDURAL MEMORY** helps you understand how stuff works. It seems to be stronger than other types of memory, which is why you may remember how to do things you haven't done for years—like riding a bike!

Scientists believe that **WALKING THROUGH A DOORWAY** may suggest a new 'scene' to the brain, so it puts away existing thoughts. That might be why people often **FORGET** why they've just walked into a room!

Some people are **MEMORY ATHLETES.** They **TRAIN THEIR BRAINS** to remember huge amounts of information, such as whole books or really long lists of numbers.

HYPERTHYMESIA is a condition where someone **REMEMBERS** almost **EVERY DETAIL** of what has happened to them throughout their life.

Most people **DON'T HAVE ANY MEMORIES** from before the age of about three or four. This may be because young brains aren't **DEVELOPED** enough to store memories for a long time.

Totally WEIRD!

Most people can remember around seven numbers at any one time. In June 2022, memory champion Syed Nabeel Hasan Rizvi memorised 30 numbers in just four seconds!

Your magnificent
MUSCLES

The shortest muscle in your body is in your **EAR** and is just **MILLIMETRES** long.

Muscles can only move the bones they are connected to in **ONE DIRECTION.** That's why muscles always **WORK IN PAIRS.** As one muscle contracts, the other relaxes.

Around 30–40% of your **BODY WEIGHT** is made up of your muscles.

Your tongue is made up of eight muscles and helps you **TALK, TASTE, EAT AND BREATHE.**

Your **FACE** is the only part of your body where the muscles are **ATTACHED DIRECTLY** to your skin.

The **LARGEST MUSCLE** is the **GLUTEUS MAXIMUS** in your bottom! It helps you move your hips and thighs around 100,000 times a day.

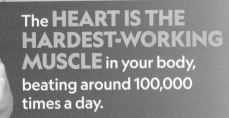

The **HEART IS THE HARDEST-WORKING MUSCLE** in your body, beating around 100,000 times a day.

You use **200 MUSCLES** to take a **SINGLE STEP!**

KISSING uses up to 34 muscles in the face, including the orbicularis oris – the muscle that **PUCKERS YOUR LIPS!**

Did you KNOW?

There's a saying that it takes a lot more muscles to frown than to smile, so it's easier to be happy. But no one knows for sure how many muscles each action uses so there's no way of proving it.

Get GLOWING

DID YOU KNOW THAT YOU GLOW?

Scientists have known for a long time that humans give off an *invisible* form of light called infrared radiation. This comes from body heat, and you can see it in pictures taken with special thermal imaging cameras.

However, infrared isn't the only type of light we send out into the world. It turns out that our bodies also emit *visible* light, the ordinary kind of light you see around you all the time. You only give off a tiny amount – 1,000 times less than you'd need to be able to see it with the naked eye. But it's there nonetheless! What's weird about this glow is that it changes throughout the day.

Scientists used super-sensitive cameras that can detect light particles (photons) to measure how much light people gave off. The light was strongest at about 10am and weakest at about 4pm. Because of this, the glow could be linked to how our metabolism works. Metabolism is the chemical reactions in the body that turn food into energy. It's lowest in the morning and reaches a peak at about four in the afternoon.

The experiments also showed that the face gives off more of a glow than the rest of the body. Because your face is more exposed to sunlight than any other part, it gets more tanned. The substance that causes skin colour is called melanin, and it's ever-so slightly fluorescent. Those fluorescent elements might be what increases the glow in people's faces.

There's a lot still to be discovered about this strange light, but that glimmer might one day help doctors figure out how healthy we are!

Did you KNOW?

Scientists think the light might be created by molecules called free radicals reacting in our bodies. It seems that it's not just humans that have it – nearly all living creatures glimmer in this way.

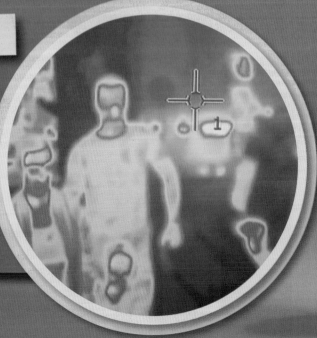

«« Thermal imaging shows infrared radiation (heat energy) as different colours.

HAIR-RAISING FACTS

FEAR FACTOR

Have you ever had **GOOSEBUMPS?** Well, that really is your hair 'standing on end'. It's one of your body's natural reflexes when you're cold or frightened. The tiny muscles near the roots of the hair on your arms, neck or other parts of your skin contract, **LIFTING UP THE HAIRS.**

MOUSTACHE RECORD

Ram Singh Chauhan holds the record for the **WORLD'S LONGEST MOUSTACHE.** He started growing it in 1970 and kept it carefully for 40 years. By that time it had reached a length of **4.29 METRES!**

HAIR EVERYWHERE

Hair can **GROW ALMOST ANYWHERE.** The only places on your body without hair follicles—the holes that hairs grow through—are the palms of your hands, the soles of your feet and your lips!

HELPFUL HAIR

Human hair is helping the environment! Cuttings from hairdressing salons have been used to create **'HAIR BOOMS'** – tubes filled with hair that are placed on beaches to **MOP UP OIL SPILLS.**

Totally WEIRD!

You have more than 100,000 hairs on your head. You lose between 50 and 100 of them every day, but new ones are always growing.

DEAD OR ALIVE?

From the hair on your head to the tufts on your toes, all the hair you can see is **DEAD!** It's alive while it's below the skin but as soon as it reaches the surface, the hair cells have died.

WIGGING IT

WIGS date back to **ANCIENT EGYPT.** Important people shaved their heads to protect them from getting lice. They wore wigs made of human hair to show their high status in society—and to protect their bald heads from the Sun!

LOOK INTO
THE EYES

BRAIN VISION ▲

You don't actually **SEE WITH YOUR EYES –** they just capture light from the world around you. This passes through your eyes, which send the information on. It's your brain that does the 'seeing'.

THE EVIL EYE

In ancient cultures, the 'evil eye' was a curse caused by a cruel stare. It probably started with the idea of envy – people glowered at others if they were jealous of them, and secretly hoped that bad things would happen to them. Special amulets were worn to ward off the curse of the evil eye.

ODD EYES

Injury or illness can change your eye colour. The musician David Bowie had a knock on the head which made the pupil of one eye permanently bigger, which made his eyes look different colours. Actor Mila Kunis had an infection that resulted in one eye being much darker than the other.

Totally WEIRD!

Brazilian Tio Chico was born with a condition called globe luxation. It means that he can pop his eyeballs out of their sockets. He can pop his eyes out a record-breaking 1.8 cm from his head and keep them out for more than 20 seconds!

SEEING COLOURS

Most people have three 'cones' in their eyes, which see red, green and blue light. These combine to make millions of different colours and shades. But some people, known as tetrachromats, can see four main colours instead of three. All of us see more shades of green than any other colour.

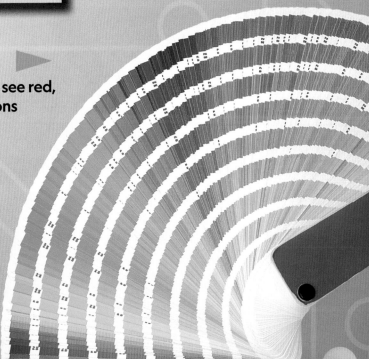

Did you KNOW?

Apart from your brain, your eyes are the most complicated structure in your whole body. They send messages to your brain, and between them, they help you work out what you are seeing.

The power of a SMILE

When we're happy, we smile. Sounds simple, right? In fact, there's much more to a smile than just showing that we're glad...

To begin with, the act of smiling actually *makes* us happier. Turning your frown upside down sends positive signals to the brain. These signals trigger the release of happy chemicals called endorphins, which make you feel good all over. The more you smile, the better you feel.

You can even trick yourself into happiness. Put on a smile even if you're sad. It might feel wrong at first, but soon your brain will start to think you're really smiling. It'll release those magic chemicals and soon your smile will be real!

Scientists have proved smiling helps people to feel less stressed out. It also gives your immune system a boost, so you're ready to fight infection and generally feel healthier. It might even help you live longer because a positive mood helps with a healthy lifestyle.

That happy feeling is infectious too. When you smile at someone, they will think that you look nice and that they can trust you. Most importantly, their body's natural response is to smile back. If they were having a bad day, you've already made them feel better!

197

Gruesomely GROSS

PARASITES are creatures that live on or even inside other living things. A type of BODY-SNATCHING BARNACLE gets inside crabs and spreads its tendrils all over it. It grows into a BIG BULGE on the crab's body. What else is inside the bulge? BABY BARNACLES!

Squirm your way over to page 210 to meet some more unpleasant parasites.

SUPER SNOT & sneeze snippets!

1. **BOGIES** from an elephant can be the same size as a human fist.

2. The speed of your **SNEEZE** is faster than a cheetah runs.

3. Around 25% of people **PICK THEIR NOSE** at least once every day.

4. Just one sneeze can shoot 100,000 **GERMS** into the air.

5. The scales of barracudas contain **MUCUS** that help increase their swimming speed.

6. A **WILD BEARDED CAPUCHIN** monkey was seen using blades of grass and sticks to get snot from her nose, which she then tasted!

7. A single **HUMAN** bogie contains around 20 calories.

8. A woman in England won a competition by **SHOOTING** the snot from her nose an incredible 6 metres!

9. Each night, **PARROTFISH** expel a blanket of mucus that they sleep under.

10. **IGUANAS** are one of the world's most sneeziest creatures.

Totally **WEIRD!**

April 23rd is World
Nose Picking Day!

Bad animal
HABITS

NOSE-PICKER

GIRAFFES don't only have very long necks—they also have very long tongues! They put them to good use for both eating and cleaning! Giraffes have been spotted using their tongue to have a good rummage up their nose!

Totally WEIRD!

Female praying mantises and black widow spiders have a horrible habit of EATING THEIR MATE once they have mated!

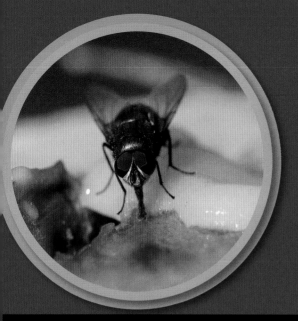

DISGUSTING DINNER HABITS

FLIES VOMIT ON YOUR FOOD!

When they land on something tasty, flies bring up a mixture of saliva and substances called enzymes. They break down the food into a soft mush that the fly laps up with its tongue.

SICK TO ITS STOMACH

If you eat something that's bad for you, you throw it up again. But did you know FROGS can't be sick? Instead, they bring up their whole stomach. While it's hanging out of their mouth, they clean off the bits of bad food with their feet, then stuff it back inside.

SALTY SNEEZES

MARINE IGUANAS live in the sea, so they get a bit bunged up with salt. But they know how to clear it out—with a powerful sneeze. The white crust these iguanas often have on their heads is where they've got caught in a shower of their own salty snot.

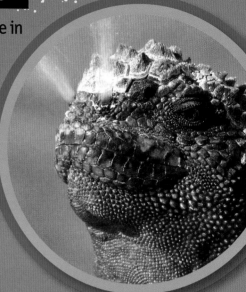

WHO NEEDS A HEAD?

COCKROACHES can survive for up to a week without their head. They breathe through tiny holes in their body, so they don't need their head to get air. Without any way of drinking, though, the cockroach will eventually die of thirst.

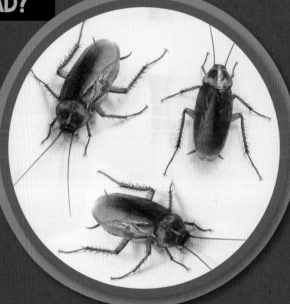

A BLOODY REACTION

SHORT-HORNED LIZARDS can squirt blood from their eyes! The blood confuses the animal attacking them. It also contains a chemical that's harmful to animals such as wolves and coyotes.

Sewer MONSTER

IN THE SEWERS BENEATH OUR CITIES, GROSS THINGS ARE SILENTLY GROWING.

FATBERGS are slimy, stinky blobs of fat, cooking oil and other items such as wet wipes that people flush down their toilets or pour down the sink. These get all gummed up together and stick to the rough surface of the sewer pipes. Slowly they grow bigger and bigger until eventually the huge mounds of gunk block the sewer tunnels and cause all sorts of problems.

Sometimes fatbergs get so big that teams of trained technicians called 'flushers' have to go into the smelly sewers to tackle them. It's a tough job because the goo hardens underground so it can't just be washed away. Workers use special power tools to break down the fatbergs into smaller pieces. Then they either remove them with buckets or slosh them away down the tunnels.

One of the biggest fatbergs ever found in London's sewers was as long as two football pitches and weighed about the same as 20 African elephants. Nicknamed Fatty McFatberg, it took a team of eight engineers several weeks to break it down into small enough pieces to dispose of safely. A piece of the fatberg is now on display in the Museum of London!

So, next time you're tempted to flush something down the loo that doesn't belong there, remember – don't feed the fatbergs!

TUDOR TOILET
ATTENDANTS

In a competition to find the grossest job ever, GROOM OF THE STOOL has to be a strong contender for first place!

The **GROOM** once had a special place in the royal court—in the toilet. It was the groom of the stool's job to help the king use the loo, to empty the pot afterwards, and maybe even to wipe the royal bottom! He was also responsible for helping the King get dressed in the morning and undressed at night, and seeing to every royal need in the bedroom and bathroom.

It sounds gross, but it wasn't all bad. The groom of the stool was considered a **HIGH-STATUS JOB** and he was an important member of the King's household. In fact, the Groom of the Stool was often the son of a nobleman and was in charge of all the other staff who attended the King in his private chambers.

It was famous Tudor King **HENRY VIII** who really made the job important. Henry had a close relationship with most of his grooms, discussing the goings-on at court or talking about things that were on his mind. After all, you must be able to trust someone who watches you pee and poo!

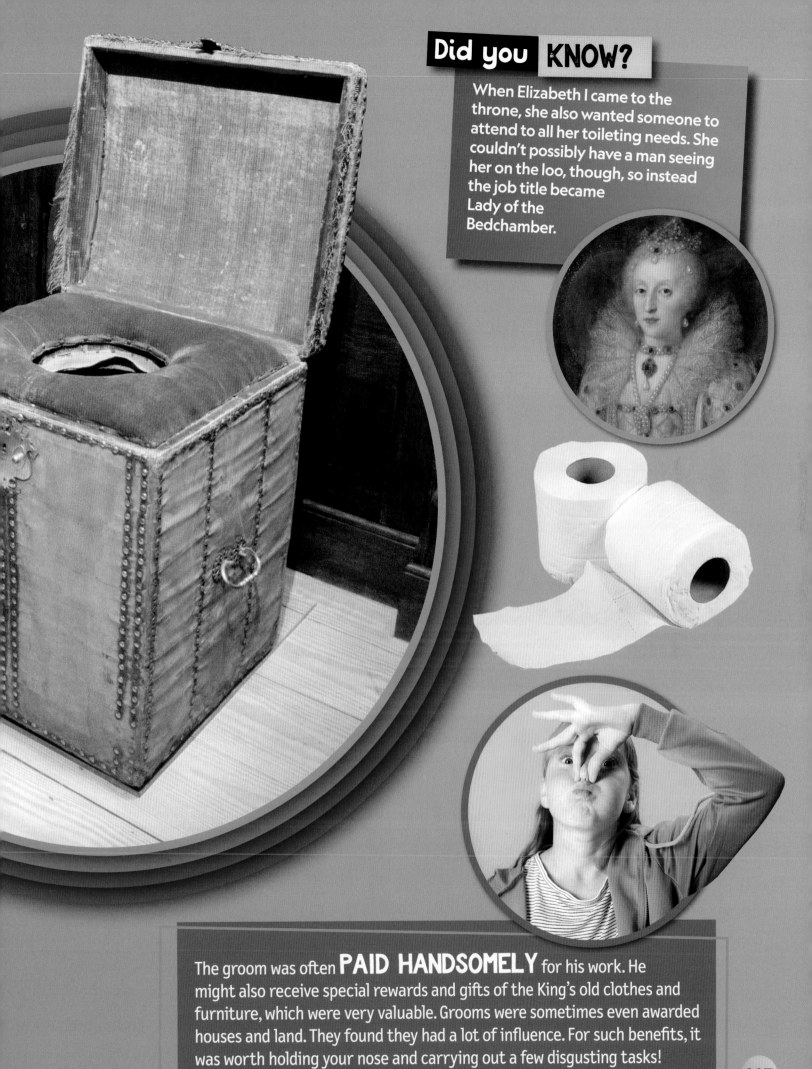

When Elizabeth I came to the throne, she also wanted someone to attend to all her toileting needs. She couldn't possibly have a man seeing her on the loo, though, so instead the job title became Lady of the Bedchamber.

The groom was often **PAID HANDSOMELY** for his work. He might also receive special rewards and gifts of the King's old clothes and furniture, which were very valuable. Grooms were sometimes even awarded houses and land. They found they had a lot of influence. For such benefits, it was worth holding your nose and carrying out a few disgusting tasks!

BLOODTHIRSTY BOOKMARK

CHARLES DICKENS apparently owned a bookmark made from the skin of a serial killer. In 1828, William Burke and his accomplice William Hare murdered 16 people in Edinburgh and sold the bodies to a doctor who used them for dissection. Burke was caught and hanged. As well as Dickens's rumoured bookmark, a pocketbook was said to be made from Burke's skin and a letter was written in his blood!

They kept WHAT?

HEART TO HEART

Frankenstein author **MARY SHELLEY** carried her dead husband's heart (or maybe his liver or kidney) around with her for 30 years! The poet Percy Bysshe Shelley drowned in 1822. The story goes that his friends cremated his body on the beach, but his heart (or whatever organ it was) didn't disappear in the flames. Mary apparently kept it until her own death in 1851.

HOW MUCH FOR THAT HAIR?

HAIR is a popular keepsake — especially if it belonged to someone famous. And it can be a good investment, too! Locks of hair have been sold at auction for thousands of pounds from historical figures such as Beethoven, Napoleon and Abraham Lincoln to singers including John Lennon and Justin Bieber.

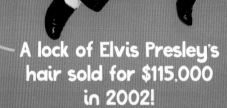

A lock of Elvis Presley's hair sold for $115,000 in 2002!

Totally WEIRD!

Saint Januarius was executed in around CE 305 but after his death a woman collected his blood. The now-dried blood is kept in Naples Cathedral, in Italy, and it's said that it sometimes mysteriously turns to liquid. Januarius is the patron saint of blood donors!

PERFECTLY PRESERVED

Russian leader **VLADIMIR LENIN'S** body was carefully preserved after he died in 1924. At first, the embalming was only going to be temporary, but as the mourners kept coming, officials had the idea to preserve Lenin's remains permanently. The body is re-embalmed regularly to stop it decomposing. It's still on display in Lenin's mausoleum in Moscow today.

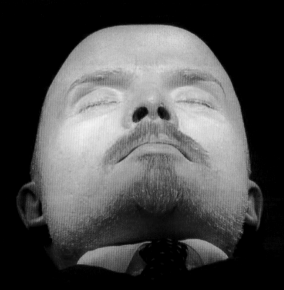

UNINVITED guests

DO YOU NEED A SCRATCH?

If so, you might have **SCABIES** – a skin condition caused by tiny **MITES** that burrow into the skin. They cause a rash and terrible itching, which is especially unbearable at night.

EATEN ALIVE

PARASITOID WASPS lay eggs inside their victims, which include caterpillars and spiders. As the eggs hatch, the baby wasps start to eat their way out of their host using **RAZOR-SHARP TEETH.**

A FULL STOMACH

Long, flat **TAPEWORMS** can live in the intestines of animals and even humans. They can grow to more than **18 METRES LONG** and can live for up to 30 years!

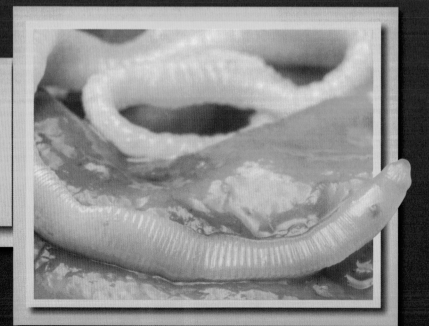

BLOODSUCKING FISH

If you're in the Amazon, watch out for a type of **CATFISH THAT FEEDS ON BLOOD.** It swims into the gills of another fish and feasts on its blood. It's no surprise that it's known as the **VAMPIRE FISH!**

The **TONGUE-EATING LOUSE** finds a fish and latches on to its tongue. It **CUTS OFF THE BLOOD SUPPLY** to the tongue so that eventually it falls off. The louse then settles in to become the fish's new tongue.

THERE'S SOMETHING IN MY EYE...

The **LOA LOA,** or **EYE WORM,** gets into humans through fly bites. People often only realise they have it when the worm reaches their eyes, where they can **FEEL IT SQUIRMING ABOUT!**

WORDS WE HATE
to hear!

1. **MAGGOTS** are small white bugs that eat rotting flesh, so it's no wonder that the word makes some people queasy.

2. There's no doubt that **PUS** is disgusting. This thick green or yellowish smelly liquid gathers in the body where there's an infection.

3. The name of the uncle in The Addams Family, **FESTER**, actually means to become infected and filled with pus. Double bleugh!

4. **BULBOUS** means big, round and bulging, but there's something about the word itself that's a bit unpleasant too!

5. The word **PHLEGM** sounds a bit like what it is – a thick, sticky substance that you cough up when you have a cold.

6. **JOWLS** are the lower part of the cheek, especially when they get all droopy and wobble about when someone talks. They're no one's favourite body part!

7. Any sentence with the word **OOZE** in it is almost certain to be describing something gross, isn't it?

8. **OINTMENT** is one of those words that just feels nasty in your mouth, but it also has horrid associations with injuries and stickiness.

Totally WEIRD!

Having a strong dislike for a particular word is called 'logomisia'. It could be based on the word's sound, meaning or its associations.

Did you KNOW?

Language experts think that certain letters make sounds that people find less appealing than others: b, g, m, o and u appear a lot in words that people don't like.

bulbous

phlegm

Everything on the environment

BISON were EXTINCT in BRITAIN for thousands of years, but a SMALL HERD of them was RECENTLY REINTRODUCED. There was even a SURPRISE addition to the family when one of the females had a BABY! The bison are AMAZING ECOSYSTEM ENGINEERS, clearing paths and stripping trees, which encourages NEW WOODLAND wildlife.

Turn to page 220 to find out more about rewilding around the world.

The rise and fall of
CLIMATE CHANGE

RISING TEMPERATURES

The last ten years have been the hottest on Earth in 125,000 years. In 2022, the heatwave across Europe was record breaking. Temperatures topped 40° Celsius in the UK for the first time ever.

RISING SEA LEVELS

Water expands as it gets warmer so, as temperatures rise, so do sea levels. All the water from melting glaciers and ice sheets is adding to the problem. The Thwaites Glacier in Antarctica has been nicknamed the 'Doomsday Glacier' because it could cause such a huge sea level rise.

SHRINKING GLACIERS

Glaciers and ice sheets in polar regions are shrinking rapidly. Greenland is losing a massive 250 billion tonnes of ice a year and Antarctica is losing around 135 billion tonnes. Overall, Earth is losing around 1 trillion tonnes of ice every year.

SHRINKING HABITATS

Shrinking Arctic sea ice means that polar bears are losing their hunting grounds. As wildfires increase, forest animals are forced to live in smaller areas. As beaches are lost to sea level rises, animals such as sea turtles have nowhere to lay their eggs.

SHRINKING FOOD SUPPLIES

Climate change and more extreme weather are affecting food supplies. In China, the 2022 drought meant that parts of the Yangtze River shrank or dried up. That not only meant less drinking water, but also no water to grow essential rice crops.

RISING DROUGHT

Extreme heat causes extreme drought. In 2022, Europe had its worst drought in 500 years. Even the trees reacted! They shed their leaves in the heat of the summer instead of autumn, to help them save water and energy.

Did you KNOW?

We can limit further damage to the environment. But to do that, we can't let global temperatures get more than 1.5° Celsius hotter than they were in the 1800s. That's why governments and scientists are all working together to tackle climate change.

CLEANING UP THE Garbage Patch

Far out in the North Pacific Ocean lies a swirling mass of litter. Known as the Great Pacific Garbage Patch (GPGP), this floating rubbish dump covers 1.6 million square kilometres – an area three times the size of France! It's mostly made up of plastic that people chuck away. There are around 80,000 tonnes of plastic in the GPGP.

Plastic is not biodegradable. It breaks down into tiny pieces, called microplastics, but it never disappears. Microplastics are harmful to sea animals and birds, as well as to humans.

In 2013, 18-year-old Dutch inventor Boyan Slat decided to tackle the problem of the GPGP head-on! He launched The Ocean Cleanup, an organisation focused on developing amazing technology to clear the world's oceans of plastic.

To clean up the GPGP, The Ocean Cleanup invented a technology it called System 001. This used a very long floating barrier that caught the plastic and moved it to a particular area, where it could be removed from the water. An improved System 002 has already replaced the original and designs for an even better System 03 are underway.

Most plastic gets into the oceans by floating down rivers, so The Ocean Cleanup realised the next step was to stop the pollution getting that far in the first place. The solution was a series of 'interceptors'. These are barriers that catch the rubbish in the rivers. Some are even linked to conveyor belts that carry the plastic back to land!

So far, the project has removed almost 200,000 kilograms of plastic from the GPGP. It's going to take a few more years to clear the whole patch, but The Ocean Cleanup is on the case!

THE OCEAN CLEANUP

Back to the WILD

BIG CAT COMEBACK

Until 2021, there had been no jaguars in the Iberá Wetlands in Argentina for 70 years. Now several of these big cats have been released into the wetlands, including mothers and their cubs. This is helping the endangered jaguars, of course, but it's also important for the ecosystem because jaguars keep populations of other animals such as caiman and capybaras under control.

Did you KNOW?

We know that to help animals survive we need to conserve their habitats. But it works the other way round, too. Animals play an important part in keeping ecosystems healthy. For example, protecting butterflies and bees helps conserve meadow habitats.

THE POWER OF THE PACK

Grey wolves in Yellowstone National Park, USA, were killed off in the 1920s. Soon after, the ecosystem began to suffer. With no predators, elk populations increased, and they ate too many trees and plants. Other creatures lost their habitats. In 1995, 14 wolves were reintroduced to Yellowstone and today there are more than 100. The ecosystem is getting back in balance!

REWILDING WILD HORSES

Przewalski's horses are small, shaggy-furred wild horses. They were once common in Mongolia, but by the 1960s they were extinct in the wild. Luckily, a few horses survived in zoos. They were bred successfully there until a herd was released back into their natural habitat. There are now over 1,000 of them—the last truly wild horses in the world.

BRING BACK THE BEAVERS!

Eurasian Beavers were hunted to extinction in the UK nearly 500 years ago. Since 2022, they have been reintroduced to parts of the country—and now they're thriving again. Amazingly, these animals also help to fight the effects of climate change because the dams they build reduce the effects of flooding and improve water quality.

Waste not, WANT NOT

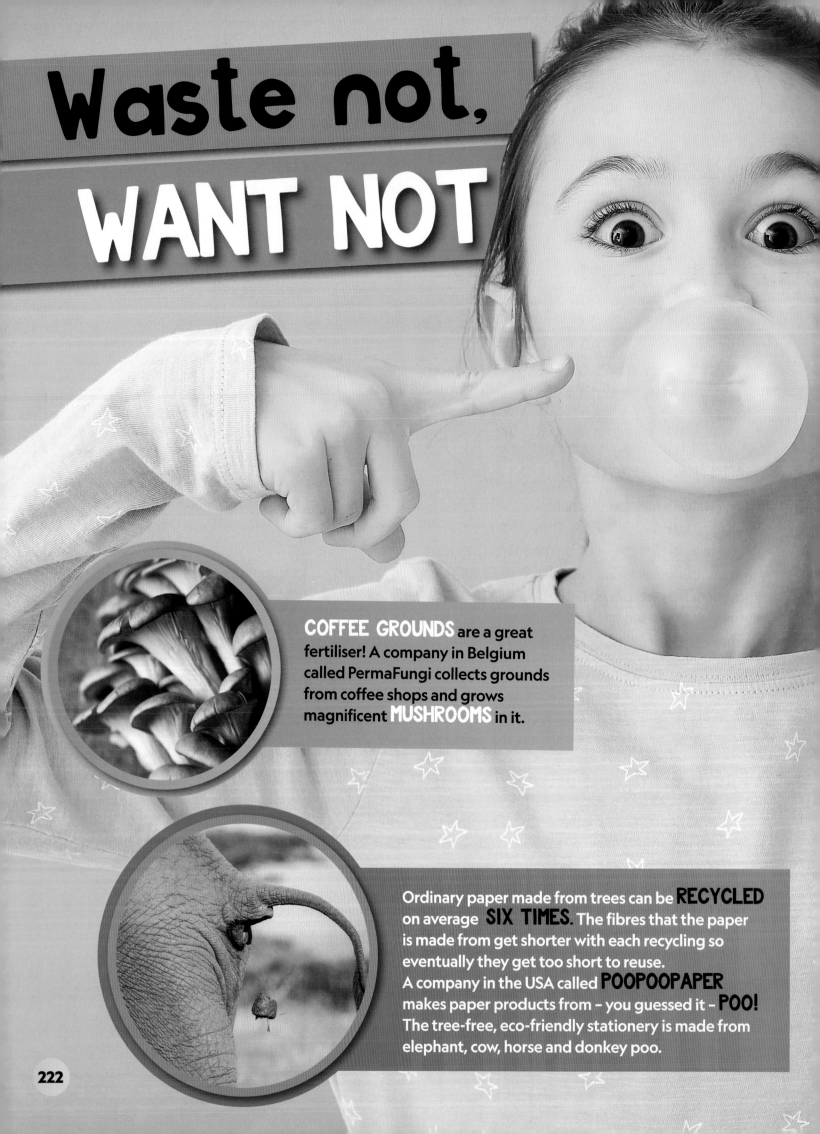

COFFEE GROUNDS are a great fertiliser! A company in Belgium called PermaFungi collects grounds from coffee shops and grows magnificent **MUSHROOMS** in it.

Ordinary paper made from trees can be **RECYCLED** on average **SIX TIMES**. The fibres that the paper is made from get shorter with each recycling so eventually they get too short to reuse.
A company in the USA called **POOPOOPAPER** makes paper products from – you guessed it – **POO!** The tree-free, eco-friendly stationery is made from elephant, cow, horse and donkey poo.

Don't drop your **CHEWED GUM** – recycle it! Old chewing gum can be made into loads of different things, from **WELLINGTON BOOTS** to **PHONE CASES** and **COFFEE CUPS.**

The first plastic toothbrushes were made in the 1930s and they quickly caught on. The problem? Toothbrushes can't be recycled, which means that just about every toothbrush anyone on Earth has ever used over the last almost 100 years still survives as plastic pollution somewhere.

In the USA, there's a company that collects **OLD SOCKS** and grinds them down into a fibre – which can then be turned into yarn to make **NEW SOCKS!**

Amazing metal **ALUMINIUM** can be recycled endlessly. So, your fizzy drinks cans can go on and on and cause hardly any waste or damage to the environment – as long as you recycle them!

A company called Cycle of Good collects inner tubes from bicycle wheels in the UK and sends them out to Malawi, Africa. There, a team of tailors turns the tubes into bags, belts, wallets and other items.

Shoe company Sanuk takes old sports mats, like **YOGA MATS,** and turns them into environmentally friendly **FLIP FLOPS!**

ECO-LIVING

ORGANIC AGRICULTURE
SEKEM in Egypt is one of the world's oldest eco-communities, set up in 1977. Farmers there use biodynamic methods. That means keeping the soil healthy without using human-made chemicals.

This house is built of bottles and tyres!

GREEN ARCHITECTURE
Earthship biotecture is an environmentally friendly style of architecture. And there's a whole community built this way in Taos, New Mexico, USA! The buildings are made from natural or recycled materials and get their electricity from solar and wind energy.

BREATHING BUILDINGS

In the Scottish ecovillage at Findhorn, buildings have 'breathing walls'. These let air move around between the inside and outside. This balances the temperature and moisture in the air, creating a healthy environment.

ECO TRANSPORT

Masdar City in the United Arab Emirates is designed to be completely green. Everything in the city aims to be powered entirely by renewable energy. It's still being built, but eventually the city aims to be totally car-free too. People will get around using shuttle buses that can drive themselves!

MULTI-PURPOSE POWER PLANT

Copenhagen in Denmark is said to be the most eco-friendly city in the world. One famous feature is CopenHill, a futuristic power plant that turns the city's waste into energy. The building is covered by one of the longest artificial ski slopes in the world!

Totally WEIRD!

In Hamburg, Germany, there's a building that's powered by algae! It grows in glass panels on the outside. Every now and then, the algae are collected and used to create a biogas that generates electricity!

A shot at
SAVING EARTH

The **EARTHSHOT PRIZE** was launched in 2021 to recognise the superheroes around the world who are trying to save our planet. For decades, nature has been shrinking as humans take over and damage more and more of the landscape. Earthshot's aim is to change that direction so that the natural world starts reclaiming its space by 2030. People have come up with some imaginative ideas to help Earthshot meets this target.

Nearly **ONE BILLION** people in the world don't have access to electricity. Nigerian Olugbenga Olubanjo had a bright idea to bring energy to poor communities by creating a solar-powered energy capsule. It's a sort of battery that people can borrow from vending machines for a small cost.

In **INDIA**, there are millions of ironing vendors—people who iron clothes on carts with ironing boards. The charcoal used to heat the irons pollutes the air and causes lung disease. To solve the problem, 14-year-old Vinisha Umashankar designed a solar-powered ironing cart!

SEAWEED.
NOT PLASTIC.

FIND OUT HOW YOU'RE HELPING THE PLANET
↓

finally a box that is truly
MADE TO BIODEGRADE

~~plastic~~ ☐   seaweed ☑

NOTPLA

Can you guess what **NOTPLA** is? Well, it's not plastic, that's for sure! It's an alternative to plastic that's made from seaweed. It can be used instead of plastic in all sorts of ways. In fact, the food delivery service Just Eat has started using Notpla for its takeaway boxes!

Did you KNOW?

There are five Earthshot categories:
- Protect and restore nature
- Clean our air
- Revive our oceans
- Build a waste-free world
- Fix our climate.

What invention can you come up with that could be in with a shot at winning one of these Earthshot prizes?

CLIMATE CHANGE and POLLUTION are

threatening coral reefs around the world. In fact, at the current rate, 90% of coral will be gone by 2050. A company in the Bahamas has worked out a way of growing coral on land—50 times faster than it grows in the sea! This could save coral from extinction.

By the numbers

PAC-MAN

CHAPTER 1

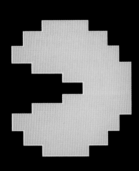

In computer game **PAC-MAN,** the **HIGHEST SCORE** you can get is **3,333,360.** To get there, you have to **MUNCH** your way through every **DOT, PILL, GHOST** and **BONUS** in the game.

Count down to page 242 to explore more gaming facts and figures.

TEN on 24

There are **24 CARATS** in 100% pure gold.

Most people have 12 pairs of **RIBS** in their rib cage, making 24 in total.

A shape that has 24 sides is called an **ICOSITETRAHEDRON** – or a 24-GON!

24 is a **SEMI-PERFECT NUMBER,** which means that if you add up some of the numbers it can be divided by, you can make 24 (1 + 2 + 3 + 4 + 6 + 8 = 24)!

In the famous **24 HOURS OF LE MANS** race, the winner is simply the car that travels furthest in 24 hours.

In **ROMAN NUMERALS,** the number 24 is written XXIV.

In **NATIONAL BASKETBALL ASSOCIATION** games, players have 24 seconds on the shot clock to try and score.

Totally WEIRD!

2024 is a leap year. Leap years happen every four years, except for end-of-century years that can't be divided by 400. So, the year 2000 was a leap year, but 1900 wasn't!

In **MILITARY TIME,** the hours are expressed in numbers up to 24. So, 4 o'clock in the afternoon is 1600 or 'sixteen-hundred hours', for example.

The traditional **CHINESE CALENDAR** is divided into **24 SOLAR TERMS** of about 15 days each, which are named after weather, the seasons, nature and crops.

Melons, rice and snails all have **24 CHROMOSOMES.**

A WORLD OF NUMBERS

19.7

The vertical (upright) distance in kilometres between the highest point on Earth—the top of Mount Everest—and the lowest point, in the Mariana Trench deep in the Pacific Ocean.

672

The telephone dialling code you need to make a call to anywhere in Antarctica, including the South Pole. There's no code for the North Pole because no one governs it!

Did you KNOW?

The average walking speed is 5 kilometres per hour. The distance all the way round Earth at its widest point is 40,075 kilometres. That means it would take about 8,015 hours, or 334 days non-stop, to walk all the way round the planet.

839

The estimated number of languages spoken in Papua New Guinea—more than any other country in the world. There are about 7,000 languages spoken across the world, but many of them are dying out as younger generations stop speaking them.

3

The number of countries that *don't* have a rectangular flag. Nepal's flag is shaped like two long triangles, one on top of the other. The flags of Switzerland and Vatican City are both square.

HUNDRED

HUNDRED

Henry Church, who died in 1860 at the age of 109, was familiarly known as "Old Hundred" and the town was named for him. He was a soldier in the British Army under Cornwallis and was captured by American troops under Gen. Lafayette.

The name of a town in West Virginia, USA. An early resident was Henry Church, who lived to the great old age of 109. Other settlers in the area nicknamed him 'Old Hundred', and the town was named in his honour.

2

The number of countries that have the letter X in their name: Mexico and Luxembourg. X is the only letter of the alphabet that doesn't come at the start of any country or territory's name.

What's on your mind?

Get your head round some facts and figures about your amazing brain.

2.5 MILLION

The number of gigabytes of memory storage space that your brain has. That's around 2,500 times more than an average computer.

1.4

The weight of the average human brain in kilograms. That's about 1/44th of a person's total weight.

100 billion

The number of brain cells you have – roughly the same as the number of galaxies there might be in the universe.

435

The speed in kilometres per hour that messages travel between neurons (brain cells). That's about half the speed of a passenger plane.

20,000

The number of words that an average 10-year-old knows. At that age, your brain is also learning around 20 new words every day.

57

The age at which people start forgetting things. You can keep your memory sharp by practising remembering random things – like the facts in this book!

10

The number of minutes it takes for your brain to forget 90% of your dreams after you wake up.

Totally WEIRD!

There are 150,000 kilometres of nerves in your brain. These allow it to control everything you do from seeing and hearing to walking, eating and breathing.

Moon MATHS

Compared to other space bodies, the Moon looks big to us. In fact, with a **DIAMETER OF 3,475 KILOMETRES,** it's the **FIFTH LARGEST** out of the 200 or so moons in the Solar System. It's **JUST OVER A QUARTER** of the size of Earth, which makes it the biggest moon relative to the size of the planet it orbits.

Our only satellite is an ancient inhabitant of the Solar System, about **4.53 BILLION YEARS OLD.** It takes **27.3 DAYS** to complete **ONE ORBIT** of Earth, but weirdly it takes **29.5 DAYS** to go through all its **PHASES** from new moon to new moon again. Daytime on the Moon lasts about **TWO WEEKS,** and temperatures reach **127 DEGREES CELSIUS –** more than hot enough to boil water. Night also lasts about **TWO WEEKS,** and temperatures then drop as low as **-173° DEGREES CELSIUS.**

The Moon is **ABOUT 384,400 KILOMETRES AWAY FROM EARTH.** So, if you set off by car and travelled at an average speed of **97 KILOMETRES PER HOUR** (about 60 miles per hour) and didn't make any food or toilet stops at all, you'd get there in about **FIVE AND A HALF MONTHS.** It's probably better to hitch a ride on a spacecraft, which reach the Moon in about **3 DAYS!**

There have been **SIX** successful crewed missions to the Moon— **APOLLO 11, 12, 14, 15, 16** and **17,** which all took place between **1969** and **1972. TWO ASTRONAUTS** from each of those missions set foot on the lunar surface—12 in all. Between them, those astronauts gathered up **382 KILOGRAMS OF ROCKS, PEBBLES, SAND AND DUST** from the Moon and brought them back to Earth.

Totally WEIRD!

The Moon is 400 times smaller than the Sun, but it's also 400 times closer to Earth. That's why the Sun and Moon look about the same size from where you're standing!

Leg COUNT

ONE... Slugs, snails and many other molluscs are **UNIPEDAL** – that is, they move on only one leg. Or, scientifically speaking, one *foot*.

TWO... Apart from humans, there aren't many creatures that only walk on two legs. It's mostly flightless birds such as penguins and ostriches that join us in the **BIPEDAL** category.

THREE... Everyone believed that there were no **TRIPEDAL** animals on Earth, until someone realised that parrots use their beaks with the same amount of force as their legs when climbing trees, like a third limb.

FOUR... You can take your pick of **QUADRUPEDAL** creatures. Most animals use four legs, including almost all mammals – around 500 billion of them – walking around on Earth!

FIVE... Some scientists claim that the kangaroo is the world's only PENTAPEDAL animal. A kangaroo's fifth 'leg' is its powerful tail, which it uses to move around.

SIX... Insects from ants and bees to butterflies and grasshoppers are all HEXAPEDAL. All six legs are attached to the thorax – the middle part of an insect's three body parts.

SEVEN... Okay, it's arms not legs, but the seven-armed starfish uses its arms for moving around so it counts as a HEPTAPEDAL animal.

Totally WEIRD!

Centipedes rarely have 100 legs! They average 35 pairs of legs but can have anywhere between 15 and 177 pairs!

EIGHT... The group of scuttling OCTOPEDAL animals is arachnids. This includes spiders, scorpions, daddy longlegs and some types of mite and tick.

239

IT ALL ADDS UP TO ANCIENT EGYPT!

2,000

The number of gods and goddesses worshipped by ancient Egyptians. Some numbers themselves were linked to the gods. For example, 3 was a sacred number associated with groups of three gods such as Osiris, Isis and Horus.

700

The approximate number of hieroglyphs in the ancient Egyptian alphabet. These 'letters' were in the form of pictures and symbols. Some of them stood for the objects they pictured, while others were sounds.

1.6

The length in kilometres of bandages used to wrap one body when it was mummified by the ancient Egyptians. The whole process took around 70 days, so people had to wait a while for the funeral!

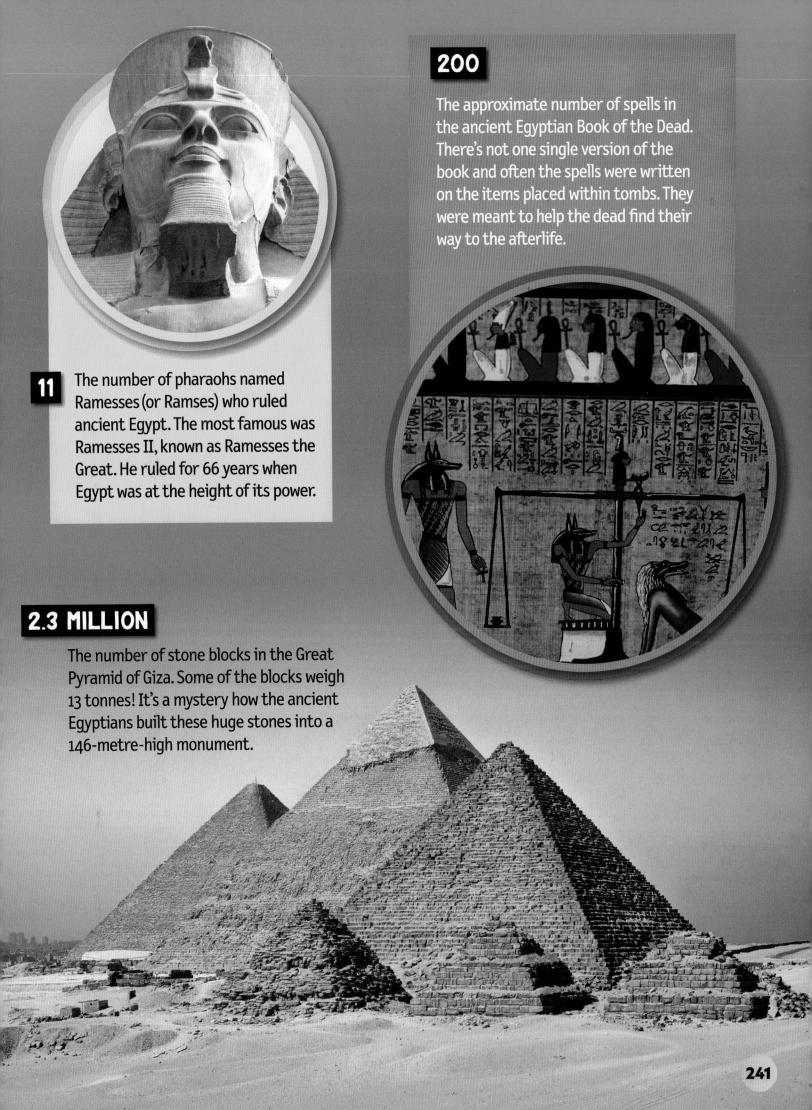

200

The approximate number of spells in the ancient Egyptian Book of the Dead. There's not one single version of the book and often the spells were written on the items placed within tombs. They were meant to help the dead find their way to the afterlife.

11 The number of pharaohs named Ramesses (or Ramses) who ruled ancient Egypt. The most famous was Ramesses II, known as Ramesses the Great. He ruled for 66 years when Egypt was at the height of its power.

2.3 MILLION

The number of stone blocks in the Great Pyramid of Giza. Some of the blocks weigh 13 tonnes! It's a mystery how the ancient Egyptians built these huge stones into a 146-metre-high monument.

Get in the GAME

One of the first video games appeared in 1958. It was called Tennis for Two and was a bit like the later game PONG.

Time is measured in ticks in the world of MINECRAFT. There are 24,000 ticks in a Minecraft day, which takes about 20 minutes to play.

CANDY CRUSH was the most-played video game in 2022, with around 2.7 billion players all over the world, trying to make their way through the game's 12,000+ levels!

Nintendo's plumber hero MARIO has appeared in over 200 games. He was first spotted more than 40 years ago in Donkey Kong, which was released in 1981.

Did you KNOW?

The Nintendo Game Boy was the first games console to be taken into space, and Tetris the first game to be played outside Earth. Russian cosmonaut Aleksandr Serebrov took them with him to the Mir Space Station in 1993.

More than 40 million players tried to get into the finals of the first FORTNITE WORLD CUP in 2019. In the end, 100 PLAYERS competed to win a £3 million prize!

243

Index

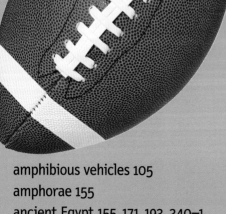

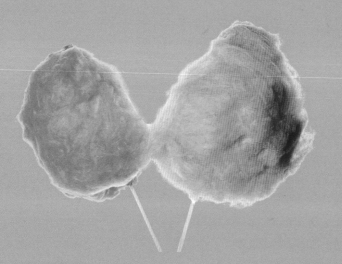

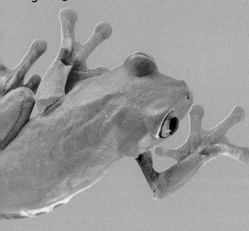

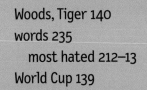

Image credits